the urban potter

A MODERN GUIDE
TO THE ANCIENT ART
OF HAND-BUILDING
BOWLS, PLATES,
POTS AND MORE

the urban potter

Emily Proctor

Photography by Sarah Weal

KYLE BOOKS

Dedication

For Lucas, Holly and David.

———————

An Hachette UK Company
www.hachette.co.uk

First published in Great Britain in 2023 by
Kyle Books, an imprint of Octopus Publishing Group Limited
Carmelite House
50 Victoria Embankment
London EC4Y 0DZ
www.kylebooks.co.uk

ISBN: 9781914239700

Distributed in the US by Hachette Book Group, 1290 Avenue
of the Americas, 4th and 5th Floors, New York, NY 10104

Distributed in Canada by Canadian Manda Group, 664
Annette St., Toronto, Ontario, Canada M6S 2C8

Publisher: Joanna Copestick
Junior Commissioning Editor: Samhita Foria
Design: Rachel Cross
Photography: Sarah Weal
Production: Peter Hunt

Printed and bound in China

10 9 8 7 6 5 4 3 2 1

Emily Elizabeth Proctor's hand-built ceramics are created in her North London studio. She uses coarse stoneware clays and natural glazes to make simple and imperfect shapes that emphasize rather than hide the handmade nature of the objects. Tool and finger marks are deliberately left behind and glazes applied irregularly to create playful and rustic wares.

After studying 3D Design at art school in Bournemouth, Emily worked in London as a stylist, buyer and creative director for ten years. Her work is almost exclusively made using ancient hand-build methods, in an attempt to slow down and reconnect with the past. The forms are designed to be simple and primitive, allowing the texture and colour of the clays and glazes to speak for themselves.

Emily saved up to leave a conventional career at age thirty-two to embark on a new lifestyle. Focusing not on capitalist markers of success like money and status but pursuing joy and wellbeing through slow-living and craft, which she continues to this day.

Contents

Introduction

'A good idea is a perfect surprise, something people didn't know they wanted until they saw it.' **Vivienne Westwood**

I picked up my first piece of clay when I was ten, when the art department at my school had a small kiln installed. The art teacher rang my parents one day to rave about this little clay boot I had made, which must have had a big impact, as I can still remember how proud that made me feel. Years later, when I was working at a furniture brand but becoming slightly disillusioned with the industry, I started to look for something more nourishing to dedicate my time to. I decided to take some ceramics classes to find out if I really had any talent, or if that sad little boot was, in fact, the limit of my abilities.

At the furniture company I was working for, we bought our ceramics from huge suppliers that mass-produced homeware in Asia. Just like in the fashion industry, new colours and styles were introduced every season to encourage people to buy more and more disposable homeware pieces. A lot of the ceramics we were importing were made to look hand-crafted but of course were being churned out in their thousands. I was concerned not only about the environmental issues surrounding 'fast homeware', but also about just how disposable and meaningless it all felt. Being around this culture of trend-driven, throwaway decor actually propelled me in the opposite direction and fuelled my decision to make my own ceramics: one-off, handmade objects that I hoped would be treasured and loved by their owners.

I've always enjoyed making things, but I could never have predicted what a profound impact pottery would have on my life. Ceramics is now my world. I wake up thinking about coffee cups and dream of candlesticks at night. It's odd that you can have almost zero engagement with something for your entire life and then, within a month of dabbling with it, realize that this was the thing that you were meant to do.

Teaching myself pottery wasn't as straightforward as I thought it would be: I wouldn't recommend ceramics as a business to anyone who wants to 'make a quick buck'. That's really not what it's about. But if you're looking for a rewarding hobby or to immerse yourself in the world of clay, I hope this book can start you on your way.

Making pots can be a welcome respite from the fast-moving and relentless nature of many other aspects of our society. We have a newly-evolved capacity for high-speed scrolling and multitasking, but ceramics demands quite the opposite: you have to slow down, concentrate and consider every movement you make. There is a meditative and soothing quality to working with clay, primarily because it's something that is almost impossible to rush. One of the most valuable and rewarding parts of ceramics is in developing an ability to concentrate and create rather than consume and discard.

My own practice was pivotal in my recovery from serious illness and the anxiety and PTSD that came with that, and I strongly believe that everyone is capable of making beautiful objects and connecting with themselves in the process. Self-expression is a powerful healing tool; no matter how stressful life gets, I know that I can pick up a chunk of clay, start pinching and restore order in my mind. It's also a great way to fill your house with twenty different iterations of a soap dish…

There seems to be this resounding myth that making studio ceramics is incredibly difficult or inaccessible. Of course, like any medium, lots of elements of it are hard; throwing pots on the wheel, for example, can take years to master, and you could spend a lifetime experimenting with glazing. But experimentation and a lifetime of learning possibilities are actually part of the fun. I want to show you that the basics of pottery are easy. Contrary to popular belief, pottery does not have to be prohibitively exclusive or expensive. For the price of a gym membership, or even through pay-as-you-go classes and courses, anyone can get involved.

Pottery as an art form is as old as civilization itself. If Stone Age people could mash together some mud with their hands and bake it in the sun to make a cup then I'm pretty sure you can too. I often glance at the shelves of freshly fired work in my shared studio space and find myself drawn to those pots made by beginners. I'm yet to see a crudely made little bowl or pot that I didn't find utterly charming.

As with all art forms, beginners often lack the self-consciousness and technique that experts can become constrained by, and they also bring a new perspective. Masters are incredibly important to any profession, of course, but collaboration, experimentation and a break with the expected or preconceived is what makes art exciting and drives it forward.

I specialize specifically in hand-building, and I've developed a style of making that is deliberately primitive and rustic. The focus is not on perfection, but imperfection,

which makes it ideal for beginners. The type of glaze and clay I use means that any mistakes you make during building will only enhance the rustic look and charm of your finished pieces – in my opinion, at least. You won't need a lot of tools or specialist equipment. Most of what you need you probably already have in your kitchen drawers. If you are a perfectionist, I want this book to help you to see that perfection is the enemy of style. I want to liberate you from its restraints and guide you to find beauty in the unusual. And if you already embrace the lure of the flawed, ugly and weird: welcome home, my friend.

I'm going to teach you how to make exciting and stylish pottery in your own home. However, once dry, most clay will need to be fired in a kiln. There are many studios you can take your pots to where they can be fired for a small charge, or you could do what I did and join a collaborative makers' studio space. I joined Turning Earth, where I was able to develop my practice among their extensive community of members and experienced technicians.

I can't overstate how transformative and encouraging being a member at Turning Earth has been to my practice. Without their support I would not have had the space, money or time to get my ceramics business off the ground. Collaborative spaces like Turning Earth help remove the barriers that often confine crafts to being short-lived hobbies or pursuits purely for the rich. It is well worth investigating what exists in your area, as these spaces can make an otherwise expensive or baffling craft seem much more attractive, accessible and affordable.

I have structured the book with the approach that your practice will eventually take you to a makers' studio set-up to make and fire your pots. As mentioned above, you could also buy clay and paint-on glazes, make the pieces at home and take your pieces to a studio where a technician will fire them for you. I have also included a section on air dry clay so you can follow any of the projects using clay that doesn't need to be fired. Air dry clay is a great way to give pottery a try at low cost, and to practise your techniques before investing in joining a studio. Air dry clay is also a fantastic way for children to get into pottery while experimenting safely.

The Basics projects will teach you the basic techniques of hand-building with a series of small pots. Moving on, the Next Level projects will help you practise and build on these skills. You will then go on to master all of these techniques and combine them to make larger, more ambitious pieces in the Hard section. I strongly recommend focusing on practising and fully understanding each section before moving on to the next, because the larger, more technical projects will be too challenging for beginners without a knowledge of the basics.

We all know after watching Patrick Swayze and Demi Moore's seductive performance in the classic Nineties' film *Ghost* that pottery is sexy AND scary. But don't be afraid, even though it's rife with slapping, squeezing, squelching and a slurry of other lip-curling innuendo possibilities, it is – more than anything – a place to explore, express yourself and have fun. And who doesn't look good in a pair of slurry-covered dungarees, I ask you? If you've watched Channel 4's amazing *The Great Pottery Throw Down,* you'll also know that it's virtually impossible to spend any time in a pottery studio without sinking to a level of humour that the finger-sucking Nigella Lawson would find 'a bit much'. I've tried, as a so-called professional ceramicist, to keep this book out of the gutter, but I failed. #youarewelcome

I am not a master ceramicist, nor a production potter, but I am a self-taught expert at what I do. Which is to say: unusual, abstract and playful studio ceramics. I hope that these projects show you how simple and rewarding ceramics can be. Armed with just this book, a few tools and a bit of practice, you may ignite a similar passion for making as I did.

Love, Emily x

Clay

Clay is, in essence, mud with special properties, and it's one of Earth's most abundant resources. The result of a chemical reaction between silicate minerals, water and micro-organisms, it's formed as rock over a really, really long period of time. This rock is eroded and washed down mountains by water, then deposited in lakes and along riverbeds. As the rock, made up of quartz, shiny mica and feldspar crystals, washes down the mountain it combines with organics and minerals like iron, sodium, calcium and magnesium along the way. The clay minerals, micro-organisms and microscopic platelets in this fine-grained soil develop pliability when wet but become hard and non-pliable once dry. Different combinations of these minerals and organics are what give each region's clay its own unique characteristics.

It's impossible to know for sure how long we have been experimenting with clay, but evidence has been found at a site known as Dolni Vestonice, in the Czech Republic, that dates as far back as 30,000 BCE. Here, unfired figurines made of clay mixed with crushed mammoth bone have been found, making it at least a Palaeolithic invention. The oldest functional pottery in the world was found in the Xianrendong Cave, in China, and dates to 18,000 BCE. In fact, pre-Neolithic pottery has been discovered to have developed independently all over the ancient world in Asia, Mesopotamia, Persia, Egypt and Mesoamerica, making pottery one of the oldest human inventions, and clay the first mineral that we changed from a natural form into a synthetic material.

The practice of making pots has evolved hand-in-hand with civilization. Its durability and abundancy means it has exerted a disproportionate influence on our understanding of the ancient past in the form of decorated pots and ancient architecture. And nearly two-thirds of the world's population live in buildings made out of clay (usually in the form of bricks). Basically, humans have been playing with clay for a really long time – long before we were smelting copper and tin to make bronze (not to mention you'd need a clay mould to pour that molten bronze into). And almost every civilization has developed its own techniques, designs and unique styles influenced by the local clay, climate and traditions of its peoples.

Modern ceramics now involves so many complicated steps that it's hard to imagine how nomadic hunter-gatherers could have just invented it independently all over the world by chance. But actually, once you understand that clay is everywhere, it makes sense that after we discovered fire it was only a matter of time before those same hunter-gatherers were sitting around their fire pit one evening and noticed that they'd baked some of the earth into a more solid state. It highlights the value of curiosity and playfulness in invention. No one can tell you what exactly was happening around those campfires 20,000 or more years ago, but I'm pretty sure it wasn't a meeting, with an agenda titled 'Ten things no nomad should live without', or 'Water, where can we store it?'. Far more likely is that Ulga picked up a bit of mud and mashed it into a buffalo shape to throw at her friend Elga

on the other side of the fire pit, and when on waking they found the fire burnt out and a little solid earthenware buffalo left behind, they thought to themselves, 'Gosh, this could be useful.'

For me, practices as ancient as pottery are sacred because traditions are a way of talking to the past. Today, when we make pots just as humans have made pots for thousands of years, we speak to our ancestors in a language they created. So in essence, when you participate in ancient traditions you are communicating directly with the past. Likewise, ceramics is a great way to speak to the future. Books sadly turn to carbon, along with film and photography from the past. Computers and e-waste will break down into poisonous micro particles. But fired earth in the form of buildings and pots can last intact for millennia, telling a story to anyone who comes after us.

EARTHENWARE, STONEWARE AND PORCELAIN

There are three main types of clay that potters use: earthenware, stoneware and porcelain. Officially, the distinction between the three is based on the different firing temperatures and absorption rate once fired (vitrification). But for the layman the notable distinctions are the texture, colour and durability.

Earthenware is the clay that we have been using the longest and is the most commonly found clay in nature. The presence of iron oxide is what gives earthenware its red, tan and brown colours. It is used for bricks, tiles, terracotta pots, oven dishes and almost any pottery product you can think of. Once fired to maturity it is still porous unless glazed, which is why you might find your outdoor terracotta pots cracked after a frosty winter (rainwater is absorbed into the terracotta and when it freezes it expands and cracks the ceramic). Earthenware

contains enough iron and impurities that it can be fired to maturity by bonfire heat (600–1200°C/1100–2200°F), hence its adoption by early humans.

So-called because of its resemblance to stone once fired, stoneware is durable and comes in a massive variety of colours, ranging from off-white and sand to dark brown and black. The use of stoneware, which fires at temperatures between 1200°C and 1300°C (2200–2375°F), was only made possible once we learned how to build higher-firing kilns. First developed in China around 1400 BCE and followed later by Korea, then Japan, wide use of stoneware wasn't adopted in Europe till much later, in 1600 CE. Stoneware is often mixed with grog to give it more texture or durability. Grog is made from pre-fired clay that has been ground down into sand-sized particles. Stoneware is in principle waterproof once fired to maturity, with an absorption rate of between 2 and 5 per cent, making it ideal for functional pieces like tableware.

Porcelain is the highest-firing of the three clays,

and with an absorption rate of 0.5–3 per cent is almost completely vitrified once fired to maturity. It is white or off-white in colour, very durable and has the fewest impurities. This is because its main ingredient, kaolinite, is the primary clay, or the 'mother', meaning that all other clays are derivatives of this parent clay. Porcelain has not travelled from its site of formation, unlike stoneware and earthenware, which have gathered impurities on their journey that give them their huge variety and unique characteristics. I largely work with stoneware, and the clays I have recommended in this book are all stonewares that should be compatible with most studio kilns or kilns for hire. But check with the kiln technician before you get started, as some earthenware clays will melt at stoneware-firing temperatures, and some higher-firing clays won't reach maturity in a low-firing kiln. I will also recommend glazes that will fire well with these clays, but the same principle applies: check with the studio, they may have standard glazes they would rather you use.

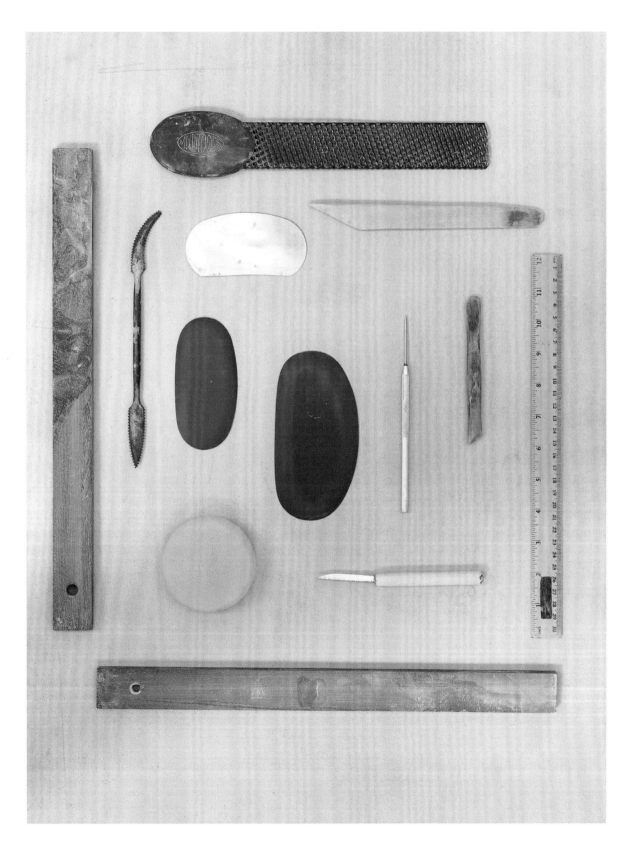

Tools

Most makers are pretty obsessed with their tools; certainly, for me, they are one of the main reasons to embark on a craft. The dream is to have an exceptional collection of hand-whittled tools perfectly organized on the studio wall. But until that day comes, my wooden box full of odd bits of wood I've whittled and tools I've bought over the years is my most valued possession.

I don't like to hang on to tools I don't use, so every one that I have is essential. I never thought I'd be the sort of person who had a favourite stick, and, like you, I used to think all sponges were pretty similar, but it turns out there is such a thing as the 'perfect sponge'.

You can end up spending an awful lot of money on pottery tools before you even get going, when in reality most of the bits you might need to be able to start can be found around the house. Indeed, lots of potters make their own tools from various found objects. Here I've recommended a reasonably priced basic kit that you can purchase along with your clay. Alternatively, I've listed possible common household or local hardware store items that you can easily substitute for the tools I use in this book. All potters have different favourite tools, so it's best to invest in proper tools once you've worked out how you want to expand your practice and what tools you want to gravitate towards.

ESSENTIAL TOOLS

This is a list of the tools – or their everyday alternatives – it's good to have prepared at the start of every project.

Water and sponge – An old washing-up sponge and a bucket of water
Used for regularly wiping down your hands, surfaces and tools to limit the spread of clay dust. You can also put all your waste clay in the bucket of water as you are working. Once you've finished, leave the bucket to sit and the clay will settle on the bottom, then you can pour out the water and re-use the clay.

Overalls – Old shirt worn back to front
Clay is very messy and some clays contain elements like manganese or tin that can stain clothes black or red. So while working with it, wear clothes that you don't mind getting stained, and wash them regularly to avoid the build-up of clay dust.

Work bench – Old wooden table
You need a large, flat, ideally wooden surface to work on. Any table or desk will do, but do be aware the minerals in clay can stain untreated surfaces, so don't work on your best table. Before I had a work bench I went to hardware stores or timber yards and asked them for offcuts of plywood to work on.

Ware board – Old chopping boards

In pottery we use ware boards to dry our work on and to move it around. These are essentially just flat pieces of wood that help to draw moisture out of the base of your pots so the base and sides dry more evenly. Rather than buying specialist boards you can just use an old chopping board. Or you could also ask for offcuts at a hardware store or timber yard. Plywood works best.

Rib – Old store/credit card

Referred to as a rib or kidney because of the shape, you can get rubber, wooden and metal ribs. They are used for smoothing, compressing or scraping clay to create texture and for blending clay together. I wouldn't start a project without a rib to hand, so it's worth investing in one. Alternatively, lots of potters actually prefer to use an old credit card.

Potters wire – Garden wire wrapped around two pencils

Potters wire is basically cheese wire, which is really useful for dividing and weighing out clay. Hold the wire straight by pulling the pencils taut on either side and slice through the clay.

Weighing scales – Kitchen scales

All the projects require you weigh out the correct amount of clay first. Doing this in advance of each project helps you to repeat the same size and shape pots and regulate drying times.

Banding wheel – Newspaper

A banding wheel is a turntable for spinning your piece around while you are working on it. I find a few pieces of newspaper folded or cut to size work well in the absence of a wheel.

EXTRAS

Wooden tools – lollipop sticks, spoons, whittled sticks, cocktail sticks, wooden ruler, spatula

Wooden tools are just shaped pieces of wood that can have all sorts of uses in pottery. They can be used to blend, compress, carve, shape and create texture on the clay. You can purchase a hand-building starter kit or just look around the house and gather together a collection of wooden things. I find a combo of lollipop sticks and old spatulas pretty much covers all the tasks I need if I have nothing else to hand.

Metal tools – Serrated knife, knife, butter knife, teaspoon, metal ruler

A knife is pretty useful for cutting slabs of clay, and a serrated knife makes short work of the scoring part of 'slip and score', which we use for slab building (see page xx). You can also use objects like teaspoons or butter knives for shaping and smoothing your pieces.

Rolling pin – Old kitchen rolling pin

For bashing lumps of clay flat and rolling out slabs.

Rolling guides – Dowel

Long wooden sticks of different widths to place either side of a slab to help you roll out clay evenly. For these projects you'll mostly be using 8mm (⅓in) rolling guides, so you could use offcuts of 8mm (⅓in) dowel from a hardware store.

Cloth – Old tea towels

I tend to wash my hands in the water bucket then wipe them straight on my overalls, which I wash regularly, but it's less messy at home to use an old rag or tea towel and wash that, to limit clay dust.

Plastic sheets – Recycled shopping bags

Potters use plastic to cover clay to control the drying process. It's really useful to have recycled plastic sheets to wrap up projects and come back to them later, or to cover parts of your project to stop them drying too quickly. Cut-up bin bags or shopping bags work really well, too.

Water spray bottle – Old cleaning spray bottle

Also useful to control the drying process, especially for big sculptures or vases. Just wash out an old spray bottle, fill it with water and spritz your clay as needed.

Terminology

Leather hard – When the clay is in a damp but stiffened stage. It can support its own weight and doesn't bend out of shape when light pressure is applied but you can indent it with your fingernail and make changes to its surface. Hand-building methods regularly require a bit of a wait for clay to become leather hard or soft leather hard before you build with or work on it.

Soft leather hard – Softer than leather hard, this is when the clay has stiffened a little but is still pliable without cracking. So you can bend and manipulate it into the shape you want but it will hold its shape more reliably than wet clay straight from the bag.

Grog – A ceramic raw material added to a clay body for durability, colour or texture. It can be made by high-firing selected clays, then grinding them down to a coarse powder with a high percentage of silica and alumina.

Greenware – The term potters use for unfired pottery.

Bone dry – Before your greenware pot can be fired it needs to be completely dry, or 'bone dry'. Test it by holding it against your cheek; if it feels cold to the touch then it still contains moisture and needs longer to dry. Bone dry ware is fragile, non-plastic and porous, so be very careful when handling it.

Firing – Once your greenware pot is bone dry the next step is to fire it. Firing is the process of heating greenware to maturity in a kiln to achieve its maximum non-porosity or hardness. Modern glazed ceramics usually go through a two-step firing process, with temperatures ranging from 600°C to 1400°C (1100–2550°F).

Bisque firing – A bisque firing is the preliminary firing prior to glazing. Once your greenware pot is bone dry it will be fired to bisque, which is typically a lower temperature than glaze firing.

Bisqueware – Once your pot has gone through its first firing it is called bisqueware. At this stage, it is porous with a chalky texture and ready to be glazed.

Glaze – A vitreous coating bonded to a ceramic by heat. After your pot has been fired to bisqueware it is ready to be glazed before its glaze firing. Glazes come ready mixed or in powder form to be mixed with water in large containers. You can also make your own ash or salt glazes, but this is a complicated science best done with guidance from an expert.

Glaze firing – Usually the second and final firing stage, during which the glaze melts and forms a vitreous coating onto the bisque-fired clay in the kiln.

Kiln – A furnace or oven for firing ceramics to maturity. The simplest form of kiln is a fire pit in which you can layer wood and pots, or you can build wood-fired kilns that require watching and feeding. Most modern urban studios will use electric kilns, since they are convenient and have a consistent temperature.

Slip and score – A technique used to bond two pieces of clay together. The potter scratches marks on the surface of the clay (score), then applies a mixture of clay and water (slip or slurry) to the scored surface.

Wedging – Very similar to kneading dough, wedging involves working the clay on a wooden or plaster surface with the palms of your hands to remove air and moisture before use. If you are using clay straight from the bag you don't really need to wedge it, but it is considered good practice and you certainly need to wedge any clay you are re-using. Hold your lump of clay in both hands and push it away from you and against the surface of the workbench at the same time. Repeat this action about ten times and the clay should spiral around itself. Then turn the clay 90 degrees and wedge it again about ten times. Turn and repeat each round of wedging roughly six to eight times.

Making slip – You can buy specialist slip for decorating and building your pots or it is relatively simple to make your own. For slab building, you need matching slip to your clay. Break about 50g (1¾oz) of the clay you are building with into ten small pieces in a cup. Add water until it nearly covers the clay and use a paintbrush to mix vigorously until you have a slurry the consistency of double (heavy) cream. Decorating slip is a little more complicated as it's important to have a smooth consistency and colour. So if you plan to do a lot of slip decorating, there are ready-mixed pots available to buy in all the colours you could desire. But making a slip using a contrasting colour clay will help you learn the basics. Leave to go leather hard a 100g (3½oz) chunk of clay of a contrasting colour to the clay you are making with. Then grate shavings onto a wooden ware board and let the clay get bone dry (this should take less than 30 minutes). Transfer the shavings to a cup with a wet sponge to reduce dust, cover with water and mix vigorously to the consistency of single (light) cream. This method takes a little longer but will create a smoother slurry for decorating with.

Cone – These are pieces of ceramic that measure both the kiln temperature reached, and the time it took to become that hot. They help you gauge whether your pottery will have been fired correctly. Cones with a '0' can be thought of as a negative numbers, for instance, 06 is lower than 05, but these are both distinct from cone 6 and cone 5.

BASICS

Pinch pot

CLAY
– Craft crank stoneware
  400g (14oz) lump

TOOLS
– Kitchen scales
– Wooden tool
– Banding wheel or
  newspaper
– Ware board
– Water and sponge

If someone told me twenty years ago that I'd one day 'pinch for a living', I'd assume they meant bottoms and that I was about to get cancelled! But actually, I've now turned pinching clay into a proper job. I love it, and it's the method I use the most in my work.

Pinching is the simplest and most ancient way to make a pot, with archaeologists dating some pinch pots back to Palaeolithic times. So just like the woolly mammoth, pinching is literally prehistoric. And it's this primitive nature that I'm attracted to. Underused these days, it fell out of fashion as the pursuit of detail and perfection came to represent wealth and good taste. But now, in the age of mass production, where you can print perfect objects at the touch of a button, there is a growing appreciation for irregular objects that are hand-crafted by people, not machines.

This project will teach you the basics of pinching and show you how simple it is to make a basic pot the ancient way. With just a lump of clay and a stick, anyone can make a completely original vessel. There is a temptation in pottery to keep finessing until your piece looks perfect, but I think the beauty of pinch pots is that they are irregular and unique, so don't worry about getting it perfect.

STEP 1:

Pat your clay into a rough sphere. Cupping the underneath of the lump of clay with one hand, push the thumb of your other hand straight down into the centre of the clay, roughly two-thirds of the way in. Don't push all the way through, leave extra clay at the bottom to form the base of your pot. Now you have the starting point of a pot.

STEP 2:

With your thumb still on the inside of the hole you created and your other hand supporting the base of the pot, squeeze your thumb and fingers of your pinching hand together. Gently pinch the surface of the clay between them and you should feel the clay get slightly thinner. Move the pot with your supporting hand, pinching the wall with your other hand as you go right round the circumference. The key is to make many small pinches in a circular motion evenly round the sides of the pot. Start from the bottom of the pot and move up the walls as you go round.

STEP 3:

After the first round of pinching you should have a small, very thick-sided pot. If the clay starts to crack here you can use your wooden tool to smooth over any cracks. Do this by holding the edge of the tool flat and dragging it softly over the clay, just as you would spread butter onto toast.

TIP: Lot of cracks might mean you're pinching too hard and expanding the walls of your pot too quickly. Or the clay might be too dry, so make sure you are working with soft clay straight from the bag.

STEP 4:

Now you want to slowly expand your small chunky pot into a thinner, larger pot. Keep pinching the clay with one hand while turning the pot with your other hand in an even, circular motion. You should be able to feel the rough thickness of the sides as you go round. Try to apply more pressure to the clay where it is thick and less where it is thin, evenly expanding the clay outward. With each revolution of pinching, the sides of your pot should gradually get thinner.

STEP 5:

Periodically smooth down any cracks that appear on the sides and rim of your pot with your wooden tool. Pay special attention to the rim, as this is where cracks are most likely to appear. Smoothing down the rim is often referred to as compressing the rim.

STEP 6:

After a few rounds of pinching you should have a rough vessel shape with walls about 1cm (½in) thick and a 2cm (¾in) thick base. Place your pot on a banding wheel or folded piece of newspaper and turn it as you push your thumb into the base to widen it out and create a flat bottom for your pot. Don't make the base or sides too thin, because the thinner your pot the more delicate and likely to crack it will be.

STEP 7:

Once you have the rough shape and thickness you want, smooth the inside and outside of your pot with your wooden tool. Then use your wooden tool to compress the rim again and leave to dry for about 20 minutes for the walls to stiffen up a bit. Check it after 20 minutes, the walls should be a bit stiffer or soft leather hard, which will allow you to give it a final pinch all around until you are satisfied with the shape. Then place on a ware board and let it dry for a further 1–2 hours or until leather hard.

STEP 8:

Once the clay is leather hard it should hold its shape while you refine the rim and sides. Smooth the rim by holding your wooden tool flat against the top and turning the pot beneath it. You can use your wooden tool to create a completely flat rim or change the angle to make a curve. Now smooth down the outside and inside of your pot while supporting it from the other side with your hand.

TIP: At this point you can experiment with all sorts of different finishing and mark-making techniques. Next time, why not make a few little pinch pots and try different techniques on each?

STEP 9:

Leave your pot to become bone dry (2–3 days) before you take it to be fired. Fire at cone 06 for 10 hours to bisqueware ready for glazing.

Glaze

To keep it simple I have used a premixed, matt cream glaze and the dipping and pouring technique. To glaze the inside, pour the glaze into the pot to the brim, leave for 2 seconds then tip it back out. For the outside, hold the pot at the base and dip it vertically into the glaze for 2 seconds, then remove. Now your pinch pot can be fired one last time at cone 8 for 10 hours.

Slab pot

CLAY
– Craft crank stoneware
  200g (7oz) lump
  500g (1lb 2oz) lump
  Matching slip

TOOLS
– Kitchen scales
– Rolling pin
– Rolling guides
– Ruler
– Rib
– Ware board
– Wooden tool
– Knife
– Serrated-edge tool
– Paintbrush
– Water and sponge

The various Mesoamerican societies left a varied cultural legacy: ornate pyramids, lively ball games and ceaseless, horrifying human sacrifice. But did you know they were also one of the few ancient civilizations to make wide use of slab pottery? The Zapotec Mesoamericans in particular made some very cool slab pots – and all this time you thought they only made tiles. Slab building is like a cross between carpentry and baking (bakentry, carpaking?). You roll out the slabs like a pastry chef, then you fix them together like a carpenter.

The most important things to remember in slab building are to allow enough drying time and to use plenty of clay. Building with freshly rolled slabs will usually lead to collapse; trying to bond clay that is too dry doesn't work either; and if you underestimate the amount of clay required, you will end up rolling out very thin slabs that inevitably crack. It's heartbreaking to see potters struggling with collapsing creations, torturing themselves working on clay that is either too wet, too dry or too thin. So like the three bears, be patient and wait until your clay is just right.

STEP 1:

Pat the 200g (7oz) chunk of clay into a rough sphere with your hands. Place the sphere on the table and use your rolling pin to bash it gently and flatten it out a bit. Then flip it over and bash it gently on the other side. You want to squash the clay with your rolling pin roughly but evenly.

STEP 2:

Flip it over again and turn it 180 degrees clockwise, then bash it evenly on both sides again. Repeat this action a few times and after a bit of bashing, turning and flipping you should have a chunky 2cm (¾in) thick disc.

STEP 3:

Use the rolling pin to roll the disc into a 7cm (2¾in) diameter, 1cm (½in) thick disc. You can use 8mm (⅓in) rolling guides here or anything long, straight and 8mm (⅓in) thick as a rolling guide to achieve an even roll. If you don't have anything like this, judging the thickness by eye is fine. Smooth down both sides with your rib and leave the clay on a ware board to go soft leather hard.

TIP: The ability to judge leather-hard clay comes with practice. The time varies depending on the water content and thickness of the clay, as well as the temperature and humidity in the room. For this project an hour should be enough but it's good practice to check by touching the clay so that you get used to the feel of leather hard clay – much like a chef understands how rare or cooked a cut of meat is through touch.

STEP 4:

Now take your 500g (1lb 2oz) piece of clay and pat it against your table on six sides to make a rough rectangular cuboid. Then use the rolling pin to bash, flip and turn it like you did the disc until the cube is roughly 2cm (¾in) thick. Then roll the cuboid into a long rectangle roughly 8mm (⅓in) thick and 8cm (3in) wide by 28cm (11in) long. Smooth down both sides with your rib and leave on a ware board with the disc slab to go soft leather hard.

TIP: If you're finding it tricky to roll out a circle or a rectangle, try using more clay to roll out a bigger piece, then trim it to size when it's soft leather hard.

STEP 5:

Once soft leather hard, check that the base (disc) and walls (rectangle) of your pot are going to fit together by gently wrapping the rectangle around the disc. Use your knife to trim the disc and rectangle slabs to size. Then on an 8cm (3in) end of the rectangle slab, hold your knife at a 45-degree angle to the table and cut along the edge of the slab (this gives you a larger surface area to bond the clay together). Flip the slab over and cut along the opposite short edge at a 45-degree angle.

STEP 6:

Now your slabs are almost ready to build with, but first you need to slip and score them. Use your serrated-edge tool to score all the edges that are going to meet, which for this pot is the round edge of the disc-shaped slab, along the long bottom edge and both short-side edges of the rectangle-shaped slab. Just score roughly, it doesn't need to be neat.

TIP: Your slabs all need to be drying at the same rate, so if you're making your own design, roughly plan out the size and shape of slabs you will need to construct your piece in advance so that you can roll them out together and have them drying at the same time. You can even sketch out your designs on paper and cut those out as templates.

STEP 7:

Now use a paintbrush to daub some slip along all the scored edges. Blob it on nice and thick, don't be shy.

TIP: Slip and scoring is important for bonding leather hard clay, but with some small pieces or clay that is still moist you can skip it and bond the clay just by squeezing it together. You could probably get away with making this small pot without slip and score by not leaving the slabs to dry as long. But we're going to learn best practice on a small pot so that you can apply this method to bigger pieces later.

STEP 8:

Wrap the rectangle slab around the disc slab and squeeze it around gently until the edges of the rectangle meet, then squeeze the edges together with your thumb and index finger. Give the base and all the joins another squeeze until the slip starts oozing out. Make sure all the meeting edges are properly squeezed together with no gaps.

STEP 9:

Take your wooden tool and, supporting the clay from behind, with your free hand drag the tool over the seams to reinforce the bond. Now that the clay is soft leather hard you can apply more pressure with your tool to bond the pieces together. Leave your pot for 1–2 hours to become leather hard.

STEP 10:

You can then use your rib to smooth all the seams down and compress the rim. Compress and smooth the bottom of your pot and scratch in your initials with a knife. Leave your pot to become bone dry (2–3 days) before you take it to be fired. Fire at cone 06 for 10 hours to bisqueware, ready for glazing.

Glaze

For this pot I have used a premixed, matt white glaze and the pouring technique. To glaze the inside, use a plastic jug to pour the glaze into the pot to the brim, leave for 2 seconds, then tip it back out. For the outside, hold the pot at the bottom, upside-down, and (with a bucket underneath to catch the run-off) pour the glaze in a random way over half the pot. Wait for that to dry, then pour more glaze over the other side. Where the glaze layers are thicker you will achieve a deeper colour. Now your slab pot can be fired one last time at cone 8 for 10 hours

Coil pot

CLAY
– Volcan medium
 stoneware
 250g (9oz) lump
 10 × 100g (3½oz) lumps

TOOLS
– Kitchen scales
– Ruler
– Knife
– Wooden tool
– Banding wheel or
 newspaper
– Rib
– Ware board
– Paddle
– Water spray bottle
– Plastic sheet
– Water and sponge

If you like squeezing clay into sausages, you're in luck – because that's coiling, baby. It's true that coiling is fun and rude. It can also seem like a laborious method, but if you go to the Atlas Mountains in Morocco, you won't believe the speed at which the makers there can erect a coil pot. Some potters in China make huge metre-tall coil pots for storing grain. They work with armfuls of clay at a time and slap it against the ground to shape it into massive coils that look like *ahem* snakes. See? Rude.

No one agrees on where the first coil pot was made, as the practice seems to have developed independently all over the ancient world. Some of the earliest-known examples of coil pots date back 15,000 years, to the Jōmon culture of Japan. In fact, coiling is nearly as ancient as pinching, and the two techniques are often used together. Coiling is excellent for making large, curvy vessels that would be a structural challenge with slabs or made at the wheel. It allows for control of the walls as you build upward, so you can use it to make pots that bulge out with less danger of them collapsing. This makes it an excellent way to make wonderfully organic pots. I like to make the coils as I go, but you can make a big batch and keep them moist in plastic if that's how you'd prefer to work.

STEP 1:

Take the 250g (9oz) chunk of clay and pat it into a sphere, then pinch it into a really thick, rough bowl, with the clay about 1cm (½in) thick all over. You don't need to spend lots of time here, leave it rough and chunky, as this is going to be the base of your pot. Leave on a ware board to firm up for 20 minutes.

TIP: I like to make the coils as I go, but you can make a big batch and keep them moist in plastic if you'd prefer. You need soft, pliable clay, fresh from the bags, so if you are making the coils one by one make sure to close the bag after you grab each lump of clay. The pot will gradually dry as you add each coil, allowing it to hold the weight of new ones, but you don't want the base drying out completely before you finish. So keep a water spray handy to spritz it from time to time and some plastic to cover it if you are going to come back to it later.

STEP 2:

Squeeze a 100g (3½oz) lump of clay into a fat sausage with your hands, then place on a flat wooden surface and roll it into a long, thin coil. As you are rolling out each coil you want to aim for them to be around 1cm (½in) thick and just under 30cm (12in) long. Cut the short edges diagonally where the ends are going to meet.

TIP: When rolling, keep your fingers wide and move your hands from the middle to the edges of the coil for an even shape. Be gentle, you want the surface of the table to shape the coil, not the pressure from your hands, and if your coils develop cracks use a slightly damp sponge to lightly moisten the work bench.

STEP 3:

Daub the rim of your base with water if it's a bit dry. Take your coil and place it in a circle onto the rim of your base. Check you are happy with the position and press it down gently all the way around while supporting the base with your free hand and squeeze the diagonal ends together.

TIP: This is a really good example of how you don't need to slip and score every time you are bonding clay together. The coils are freshly rolled and the base isn't leather hard yet, so there's enough moisture in the clay for it to bond. If the coil or rim is dry, daub it with water.

STEP 4:

Use your wooden tool to blend the coil to the base. Drag the flat edge of the tool over the coil downward into the base. Go all the way around the pot like this, blending a bit of the coil at a time on the inside and the outside of the pot.

TIP: If you don't have a banding wheel, put your pot on a folded piece of newspaper and use that to turn it easily around.

STEP 5:

If you want the sides of your pot to get wider use a tiny bit more clay to make the next coil and roll it slightly longer, then fix it lightly to the outside of the previous coil rather than on top. If you want the walls to get narrower, use less clay and roll your coil slightly shorter, then fix it lightly to the inside of the previous coil. With the pot pictured, I go gradually wider for three coils, narrower for three coils, then wider again for three more.

STEP 6:

Repeat steps 2 through 4 with the remaining nine lumps of clay and you will slowly see your pot getting taller. If you don't feel confident making the walls widen and narrow, that's no problem, just make a straight pot first time round by placing coils of the same length directly on top of one another.

TIP: Be aware that the structure of the base does need to support whatever you build on top, and this is limited by weight and balance. So try not to make your pot too top-heavy.

STEP 7:

Use your rib periodically to smooth down any cracks and compress the rim. You can also gently pat the sides of the pot with your paddle to compress the clay and adjust the shape.

STEP 8:

Once you have reached the height and shape you like, you can refine the rim and smooth down any cracks with your rib. Compress and smooth the bottom of your pot and scratch your initials in with a knife. Leave on a ware board to go bone dry (2–3 days) before you take it to be fired. Fire at cone 06 for 10 hours to bisqueware ready for glazing.

Glaze

For this pot I have used two glazes, a matt black and a shiny black, applied with the dipping technique. To glaze the inside, use a plastic jug to pour the shiny black glaze into the pot to the brim, leave for 2 seconds, then tip it back out. To glaze the outside, hold the pot at the bottom, upside down, and dip the pot into the matt-black glaze two-thirds of the way down for 2 seconds. Wait for this to dry, then dip it into the shiny black glaze one-third of the way in for 2 seconds. Now your pot can be fired one last time at cone 8 for 10 hours.

Hump bowl

CLAY
– Craft crank stoneware
   800g (1¾lb) lump

TOOLS
– Kitchen scales
– Rolling pin
– 8mm rolling guides
– Ruler
– Ware board
– Bowl
– Plastic sheet
– Scissors
– Newspaper
– Rib
– Knife
– Water and sponge

'What day is it? Hump day!' I shout every time I get my trusty hump moulds out (even when it's NOT a Wednesday). These handy tools are shaped convexly, as opposed to their concave sisters, the slump mould. Utilizing these bad boys can feel like using a cheat code in pottery, but actually it's a great way for experts to make a form quickly and repeatedly so they have more time to focus on the decoration. If you're a beginner, you'll also discover that hump moulds are invaluable for building confidence early on. After all, anyone can roll out a slab.

Ideally for this you would buy or make a plaster or wooden hump mould, but I find that a plastic bag, some newspaper and any bowl that you have lying around works just fine. If you have an old wooden bowl that you aren't going to use for anything else, you can do away with the plastic and newspaper.

Hand-building using drape moulds is quicker than pinching and coiling and useful if you want to make the exact same shape several times (a tableware set, for example). I tend to use drape moulds for really large bowls, too. For your first attempt use a shallow bowl – the deeper the bowl the more difficult it is to mould the clay onto it. Likewise, 8mm (⅓in) is a rather chunky bowl, but as with coiling and pinching, start chunky to give yourself a better chance of success.

STEP 1:

Pat the clay into a rough cylinder with your hands. On a wooden surface, bash the cylinder on both sides with your rolling pin until you have a 2cm (¾in) thick disc. Then roll out the disc into a 22cm (8½in) diameter by 8mm (⅓in) thick circle. You can use 8mm (⅓in) rolling guides to achieve an even roll or just go by eye. Leave your disc of clay to stiffen on your ware board for 20 minutes.

TIP: When you are rolling out clay you will get the most even results by going slowly and turning the clay over and around several times as you roll.

STEP 2:

Now take the bowl you are using as a mould and turn it upside down. Cut a circle out of your plastic that is 6cm (2½in) larger than your bowl. Wrap the plastic over your bowl and tuck it underneath. Then take a piece of newspaper and wrap that over the plastic and the mould and tuck the edges under, too. Try to get the surface of the newspaper as smooth as you can.

STEP 3:

Return to your circular slab of clay and pick it up carefully with both hands. Drape your clay slab over the mould and gently pat it down. The clay will naturally want to buckle as you pat it down, so take your time with this. Work your way around the bowl, patting it down gently until it has taken on the shape of the mould.

STEP 4:

Once you've shaped the clay over the mould, use your rib to smooth down the outside of your bowl all over and leave it to go leather hard – between 1 and 2 hours depending on the temperature and humidity of your room. Check the clay by lifting up the edge slightly, if the clay bends at the edges it's not ready, but if the whole bowl starts to lift, it's ready.

STEP 5:

Once leather hard, use the plastic to lift the clay bowl off the mould and carefully put it the right way up on a ware board, then peel off the newspaper. Use your rib to smooth the inside surface of the bowl while supporting the sides with your other hand. You can turn and smooth the bowl using a banding wheel or newspaper.

STEP 6:

Now you can trim the edge of the bowl with your knife, then compact it down with your rib. Or you can leave the rim rough and natural.

STEP 7:

Smooth down the bottom of your bowl and scratch in your initials with a knife. Leave it on a ware board to go bone dry (2–3 days) before you take it to be fired. Fire at cone 06 for 10 hours to bisqueware ready for glazing.

Glaze

For this bowl I have used a matt white glaze and the pouring technique. Hold your bowl sideways over the glaze bucket and use a jug to pour the glaze over two-thirds of the bowl. Leave this to dry, then hold the glazed side of the bowl and pour glaze over the other side. Where the glaze is layered or thicker, the colour will be deeper. Now your bowl can be fired one last time at cone 8 for 10 hours.

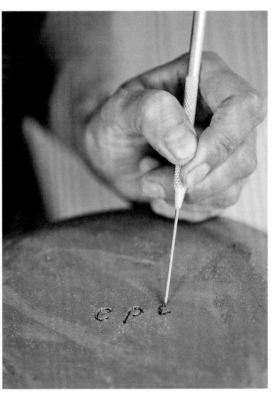

Carved pot

CLAY
– Craft crank stoneware
  6 × 500g (1lb 2oz) lumps

TOOLS
– Kitchen scales
– Knife
– Rib
– Ware board
– Cheese grater
– Carving tools or a pencil
– Water and sponge

When I was small I used to watch my dad (Chas) carve apples with a knife. I was never allowed to join in the fun, though. Apparently a four-year-old isn't to be trusted with weapons, even if it is to make a vegetable stamp. But as a thirty-six-year-old absolute legend I can now legally buy as many knives as I like, and nothing makes me feel more grown up than carving through a block of clay with my very own knife. So, screw you, Chas – but also, thanks for keeping me safe…!

Carving is a great way to achieve an impressive finish with relatively little effort. I'm going to show you a few different carving techniques that I like to use. Once you've understood the concept, the possibilities are endless. I find that the tool you choose is often what dictates the style you end up with. And a carving tool can be anything – an interestingly shaped stick you find in the park, an old butter knife, a spoon or even a cheese grater. For this project you are going to start with few really chunky little pinch pots that you've left to go leather hard, ready to try a few different carving techniques.

STEP 1:

Start by making six really chunky little pinch pots (see Pinch pot, page 26) each from a 500g (1lb 2oz) lump of clay. I would make the walls of your pinch pots around 2cm (¾in) thick so you have plenty of clay to carve away. Compress the rim with your rib, then leave them on a ware board for around 2–3 hours to go leather hard.

STEP 2:

Once the first pot is leather hard, take your cheese grater and use it to create flat edges on your pot; I've made mine into a cube by grating five sides and the rim flat. You can then use different tools to test out different finishes on each side. Holding your metal rib flat against the surface of the clay and pulling it across, for example, will compress the clay and create a smooth finish. Whereas if you hold the metal rib at a right angle to the clay surface and pull it across, it will scrape clay away and therefore create a rough surface. You can have a look around the house for edges that you think might create an interesting surface and give those a try, too. If you don't like any of the finishes, just grate it off!

TIP: On my cube I've left some grated surfaces, some smooth and some rough. This way I can see how the different finishes look when the pot is fired. Later I can also see how the glaze takes to each surface.

STEP 3:

With your second pot, use the cheese grater again but grate randomly to make lots of flat edges. You could make a symmetrical hexagon or a completely asymmetrical random shape. I've made a random shape and then smoothed down the edges with my plastic rib, then I've taken a sponge over the whole piece to wipe away some of the clay and reveal the grog.

TIP: Put all the shavings from your carving into a bowl of water immediately, before they go bone dry and create clay dust.

STEP 4:

Let's add to your second pot as well as take away. Roll up four little balls of clay (about 10g [⅓oz] each, about 2cm (¾in) in diameter) and leave them to go leather hard while you carve your other pots. After about 30 minutes, or when they are leather hard, slip and score them to this pot in a spot you think looks good. You can then use the grater or knife to carve angles onto these, too, so they match the rest of the pot.

STEP 5:

For the third pot, let's use a knife to carve pieces out of it. Hold your pot in one hand and your knife in the other, with the sharp edge facing away from you. Then carve chunks out of the surface of the pot – you will see that unlike the cheese grater, where you were making flat surfaces, a pointy tool can create indents. For this method I like to just

carve out random chunks to make an organic shape. You can, however, make a uniform pattern by making the exact same cuts while turning the pot around in your hand.

TIP: If you're working with children, give them a butter knife or teaspoon for this so they don't cut themselves.

STEP 6:

On the fourth pot we are going to carve an inlaid pattern, which we can use to glaze into after it is bisque-fired. There are plenty of pottery carving tools you can buy for this if you like the method, but for now an old pencil for fine detail or a teaspoon for larger detail will work just as well. I'm going to carve in a random abstract pattern because that's the style I like.

TIP: If you want a bit of inspiration, search ceramic inlay online or go outside and find a flower or leaf to trace around.

STEP 7:

On the fifth pot, let's just carve some holes straight through it. This is great for candle holders because the light flickers through the holes. You can use a knife for this or a pencil, it depends what shape hole you want to make. I've made matching abstract-shaped holes in mine and added some notches in the rim. Then I'm using a teaspoon to carve more clay out of the middle so that this pot can fit a little candle inside.

STEP 8:

Let's use the sixth pot to apply a texture. So go on another hunt for a textured surface. You might have an ornament, some textured fabric or a plant. Roll the pot over your texture and it should imprint on the side. I found the bottom of an old Japanese brush made interesting repeated markings.

STEP 9:

Smooth down the bottoms of your pots and scratch in your initials with a knife. Leave on a ware board to go bone dry (3–5 days) before you take them to be fired. Fire at cone 06 for 10 hours to bisqueware ready for glazing.

Glaze

I have used matt peach and matt black glazes and the dipping method. Apply wax resist to the bottoms of your pots and wax resist to any other parts of the pot you don't want the glaze to be, the inlaid pattern or the rim for example. Using tongs or your hand dip the whole pot into the glaze bucket with the top of the pot facing up to prevent trapped air, hold for 2 seconds and lift out and wait to dry. Then I have used a wet sponge to wipe away a little glaze to reveal some of the bare clay. On the inlaid pot, wipe off all the glaze that's not in the carved, inlaid parts of the pot. Now your pots can be fired one last time at cone 8 for 10 hours

Slip pot

CLAY
– Volcan medium
  stoneware
  3 × 400g (14oz) lumps
  Contrasting slip (white)

TOOLS
– Kitchen scales
– Metal rib
– Soft-bristled paintbrush
– Ware board
– Banding wheel and
  newspaper
– Scissors
– Wooden tool
– Small paintbrush
  (optional)
– Knife, carving tool or
  spoon
– Water and sponge

Slippery by name and slippery by nature. Slip is just clay with a high water content. You can paint slip onto the surface of leather hard clay for decoration or use it to join pieces of clay together. It's important when using slip that your pot has gone properly leather hard, because, as I say, it's slippery. If your pot isn't dry enough the slip and clay will mix together and give you a murky finish. If the pot is too dry, however, the slip might flake off as it dries or seep into your pot, causing it to crack.

You can either make your own slip by submerging broken-up bone dry clay in water (as described on page 23), or buy a ready-made pot of slip in a contrasting colour to your clay body. I'm going to show you three of my preferred decorating techniques using slip, but there are many, so if you enjoy using slip it's worth searching slip decoration online to get inspired by all the cool ways you can use it.

STEP 1:

Make three small chunky pots using any of the methods from the first five projects. They only need to be rough little pots each made of 400g (14oz) of clay. Smooth down the surface of your pots and compact the rims with your rib, then leave them on a ware board to go leather hard.

STEP 2:

Once leather hard, use a paintbrush to apply a thin layer of slip onto the entire outer surface of the first pot. You need to do this gently, because if you press down too hard you will disturb the clay underneath and the colours will start to mix. If you apply the slip too thickly, the water from the slip will penetrate and expand the pot. Put the pot on a piece of newspaper or a banding wheel so that you can turn the pot as you paint. Leave the pot to dry for around 30 minutes, then paint another layer of slip and leave to dry again.

STEP 3:

For the second pot we are going to use newspaper stencils. Cut out some pieces of newspaper in a simple shape and brush them with a bit of water. Then place them onto the sides of the pot in a random pattern and leave to dry for a couple of minutes. Paint two layers of slip over the top of the newspaper and the whole pot, like you did in step 2.

STEP 4:

The third pot will be decorated freehand with a pattern. Use a smaller brush if you want to make small marks and remember slip can be drippy, so try not to load your brush with too much. Leave the first layer of pattern to dry, then carefully paint another layer on top. I always apply a couple of layers of slip to ensure I achieve a solid colour on firing.

STEP 5:

While the other pots are drying, return to the first pot and, using a knife, carving tool or even a spoon, carve through the slip down to the clay underneath. The sgraffito ('scratched') technique is like etching, you are scratching away a layer of colour to reveal a contrasting colour underneath. It gives you great control over the pattern you want to make and you can achieve incredible detail. In the pot pictured I've just carved a simple pattern, but feel free to experiment with more detail, words or illustrations.

STEP 6:

Now return to the second pot to remove your stencils. Make sure the slip has dried, then use the tip of your knife to gently pull up an edge of the newspaper and slowly pull it away from the pot. This should reveal the contrasting clay underneath.

TIP: Make sure you take off all the pieces of newspaper and don't leave any behind!

STEP 7:

Check you are happy with the finish on all three pots – you can apply more slip to amend any bits you're not happy with, but don't wipe the slip with a sponge because you will smudge the colour. If you've accidently got some clay or slip where you don't want it, it's best to remove it when it's dry, by gently scraping it with the straight edge of a metal rib or knife.

STEP 8:

Compress the rims and smooth down the bottoms of your pots. Scratch your initials into the bottom with a knife and leave on a ware board to go bone dry (2–3 days) before you take them to be fired. Fire at cone 06 for 10 hours to bisqueware ready for glazing.

Glaze

I have used a matt white glaze only on the inside of these pots because I really like the matt bare clay and slip finish. If you want a shiny finish dip the pot in a thin layer of transparent glaze. Pour the glaze into the pots with a jug, leave for 2 seconds, then pour out. Now your pots can be fired one last time at cone 8 for 10 hours.

Glazing

Some potters don't like glazing, and I can understand why. You spend hours working lovingly on a pot, waiting for it to dry, baking it for hours, then you can mess it all up by choosing the wrong glaze. That's why I keep my glazing to relatively simple, neutral colours. Then the most angry that I can get with myself is saying 'Why did you glaze with matt black and not shiny black? You reckless fool!' I think the fact that I've removed a lot of the choice means I actually enjoy glazing. It's like painting with glass; I like the action of pouring the glaze and the way it dries to a sumptuous pastel powder on bisqueware. I even quite like it when it goes wrong, because an unexpected mistake can lead to something exciting and new that you would never have thought of trying.

Glaze is a glassy-looking or vitreous layer fused to pottery during firing that is used to decorate the ceramic or render it non-porous and more durable. Self-glazing pottery in the form of low-firing 'stonepaste' or 'fritware' has actually been around since 11,000 BCE in Iran, East Asia and Egypt. And a form of glazed brick goes back to the Elamite Temple at Chogha Zanbil, Iran, which has been dated to 13,000 BCE. Glazing on true pottery, however, is a relatively modern technique, and it wasn't made possible until the advent of high-firing kilns in China and the Middle East in around 1500 BCE. Since the kilns were wood-fired, the first development came when potters noticed that ash from the fire melted at high temperatures on their pots, creating a glassy-looking finish. Experimenting with ash from different woods

mixed with water led to varied reactions on the surface of the pots. Later, salt, feldspar, tin and lead were all used in glaze mixes, achieving an enormous range of results.

Today, after years of experimentation and development, the colours and finishes available to potters are vast. Anyone delving deep into the world of glazing will end up learning a lot about chemistry. In fact, you could write several books on the chemistry of glazing, which many people have, so you don't need me weighing in on that noise. But it's important to know that the type of kiln, clay body, firing speed, firing temperature, position of the pot in the kiln and impurities in the clay and glaze can all dramatically affect the outcome of the finished pot. So try to embrace the fact that it's almost impossible to achieve the same finish every time. In my work I actively use techniques that encourage the unpredictable patterns, marks and toasting produced in the firing process.

Most studio potters will embark on pretty thorough glaze testing in their own studios to ensure their glaze mixes come out right. To keep it simple for you I'll recommend some really reliable paint-on or powder glazes that will be compatible with most studios, but do check with the studio technicians first. Also, rather than listing all the various glazing techniques, I'm going to show you a handful of basic techniques that I use regularly. Each project in the book also has a brief description about how I have glazed that piece specifically. Then you can refer back to this section and follow the more detailed steps.

CLAY
– Bisque-fired pots from
   the first six projects

TOOLS
– Glaze
– Large container
– Tongs
– Wax resist
– Wooden stick/spatula
– Jug
– Rib
– Paintbrush
– Water and sponge

For dipping and pouring you need a large quantity of glaze in a container larger than the pot you are going to be dipping into it. If you join a shared studio, chances are they'll have some ready-mixed studio glazes in large buckets for you to use. One way to dip a pot is by using tongs to dip the entire piece into the glaze. This is the easiest way to achieve an even glaze all over, but you have to wipe the glaze off the bottom or paint the bottom with wax resist before you dip.

Another dipping method starts by pouring glaze inside the pot first, then hand-dipping the outside of the pot upside down into the bucket. This way you don't have to wipe the bottom but you do need be able to hold onto the bottom of your pot, so this doesn't work that well for plates or bowls.

Then there is my favourite, pour-over glazing, which you can use for any vessel really and which creates unpredictable organic patterns with each additional layer of glaze. Pour-over literally involves filling a jug with glaze, holding your bisque-fired pot underneath and pouring the glaze over it. You don't need quite as much glaze for this but you will need to place a large plastic container underneath it to catch the glaze.

Paint-on glaze needs three layers and is therefore more time consuming, but you can be really accurate or decorative with your glaze application. This comes in handy pint-size pots.

Glaze materials are mixed with water and all the heavy materials settle on the bottom of the bucket or pot when it's not being used, and if you don't mix them all together thoroughly the glaze won't fire as it's meant to. So make sure you use a long wooden stick to scrape all the sediment off the bottom of the bucket or pot and mix it up well before application.

Glaze turns into a liquid in the kiln and can run if it's too thick or too close to the base, which can fuse your pot to the kiln shelf or drip onto other potters' work, resulting in angry kiln technicians and studio pals. The runniness and therefore best thickness for each glaze can vary, so check with the technicians in your studio or go by the packet instructions. Any glaze on the bottom of your pot will also fuse it to the kiln shelf, so it's a good rule of thumb in glazing (and in life really) to always make sure your bottom is thoroughly wiped clean.

You can experiment with layering different glazes on top of each other and the mixing of the glazes can create all sorts of amazing effects. Or with paint-on glaze you can use a few colours to paint a picture or a pattern. However, the outcome of these experiments can be unpredictable, so it's good to try a few test tiles first. Also, ideally you want to be mixing glazes that fire to the same temperature. If you are buying your own glazes, check with the studio or kiln that you are hiring what glaze brands they use so that you apply a compatible one.

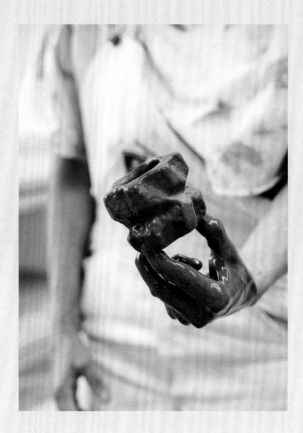

Dipping with tongs

Paint the bottom of your pot with wax resist and wait for it to dry. Make sure you are holding the pot securely with the tongs, then dip the whole piece into the bucket until it is entirely under the glaze. Dip it the right way up so there's no captured air and the glaze covers the whole pot. Hold the pot under for 2–4 seconds, depending on how thick you would like the glaze to be. Carefully lift the pot out of the glaze and put it on the bench to dry. In a couple of minutes the glaze should be dry enough that you can handle the pot. Use a damp sponge to wipe any excess glaze off the bottom of your pot.

Hand-dipping

Use the jug to pour glaze into your pot right to the top. Leave for 2–4 seconds, then carefully pour the glaze out back into the bucket. Wipe any unwanted drips off the side of your pot with a damp sponge, then place it on the bench to dry for a couple of minutes. Once dry, hold the pot upside down with your fingers and thumb at the base and dip the pot into the bucket as far as you would like it to be

glazed to. You are using the air captured in the pot to stop the glaze going inside, so make sure you hold it level as you dip. Hold for 2–4 seconds then lift out and swirl your wrist to rotate the pot over the bucket, letting any excess glaze drip off evenly. Hold it over the bucket for 20 seconds, then turn it the right way up and leave it on the bench to dry.

Pour over

Use the jug to pour glaze into your pot to the top. Leave for 2–4 seconds, then carefully pour the glaze back into the bucket. Wipe any unwanted drips off the side of your pot with a damp sponge, then place it on the bench to dry for a couple of minutes (for plates and shallow bowls you can skip this first bit). Fill the jug with glaze again and hold the jug and your pot upside down or plate sideways over the glaze bucket. With one slow confident sweep, pour the glaze in a steady stream over your pot. I usually rotate the pot or plate as I'm pouring to get more coverage in one sweep. This method can take a little time to build up confidence, so practise on a plastic pot first to get the action right. Leave on the bench to dry for 2 minutes, then hold

the side of the pot you have glazed and do another pouring sweep, covering most of the rest of the pot and some of the now-dried glaze to create layers. Wait for any drips to come off into the glaze bucket, then leave on the bench to dry. Doing two or three sweeps should usually give you the coverage you need, don't build up more than two layers of glaze in any one spot because it will be too thick.

Paint-on glaze

Take a soft-bristled brush and load it with glaze, then hold it for a second over the bucket to let any excess drip off. Then paint the glaze onto the pot in a confident but gentle brushstroke. You are not aiming to spread the glaze out thin, as you would with wall paint, it's more like how you might ice a cake. You'll find the dry bisqueware soaks up the glaze quickly, so load the brush with more glaze for every stroke. Paint the glaze wherever you want it to go, leave it to dry, then paint on another two layers.

Inlay

Find the pot into which you put an inlaid pattern in the carving project (see page 40). Use the paint-on or dipping method to glaze the whole pot, then use a slightly damp sponge to wipe away the glaze from the surface of the pot that isn't inlaid. Alternatively, you can paint wax resist into your inlaid pattern and then dip or paint the glaze on to achieve the reverse effect.

Wax resist

Wherever wax resist is applied, it will stop glaze adhering to your bisque-fired piece, then will burn off in the kiln. You can apply it to any area of the pot where you want to the clay to remain bare. It's useful for applying to the bottom of pots and plates so that you can just dip the whole piece using tongs. Or you can use it to draw patterns on your pots and glaze over the top, then when they are fired the wax will burn off, leaving raw clay and a pattern behind.

Air dry clay

– Acrylic paint colours
– Paintbrush
– Clear sealant

If you find that using a kiln is a barrier for you to start playing with clay, why not try air dry clay instead?

Air dry clay is cheap, doesn't need baking, is safe for kids and requires the exact same skills you would need to learn to work with stoneware. You can use air dry clay for all the projects in this book by following the steps right up to before they go to be bisque-fired. At that point, follow the steps laid out here.

STEP 1:

Wait for your work to go bone dry.

STEP 2:

Choose the acrylic paint colours with which you want to decorate your piece. Use a paintbrush to paint the piece to your liking and wait for it to dry. The benefit of air dry clay is that you can paint onto it in layers or using incredible detail without worrying about time constraints or what the final colour is going to be.

STEP 3:

Once dry, paint with a couple of layers of clear sealant inside and out.

PROJECTS

NEXT LEVEL

Carved candle holders

CLAY
– Craft crank stoneware
  2 × 1kg (2¼lb) lumps

TOOLS
– Kitchen scales
– Knife
– Ware board
– Dinner candle
– Tea light
– Carving tools
– Rib
– Cheese grater
– Water and sponge

Traditional candle holders took a real hit when scented candles came out. But now that we all know scented candles are bad for you (oh, hadn't you heard?) it's time to get on the beeswax dinner-candle train – all aboard! These candle holders are so easy to make I don't understand why we don't all have loads of them. Imagine how smug you'll feel at your intimate candlelit dinner party when a friend asks where you purchased your delightful candle holders. 'Oh, these old things? I carved them myself.'

In this, the first of the intermediate-level projects, you're going to expand on your carving and decorating skills. As a sneaky bonus, these candle holders are reversible and flip over to hold tea lights on the other side for slightly less formal occasions, like a bath.

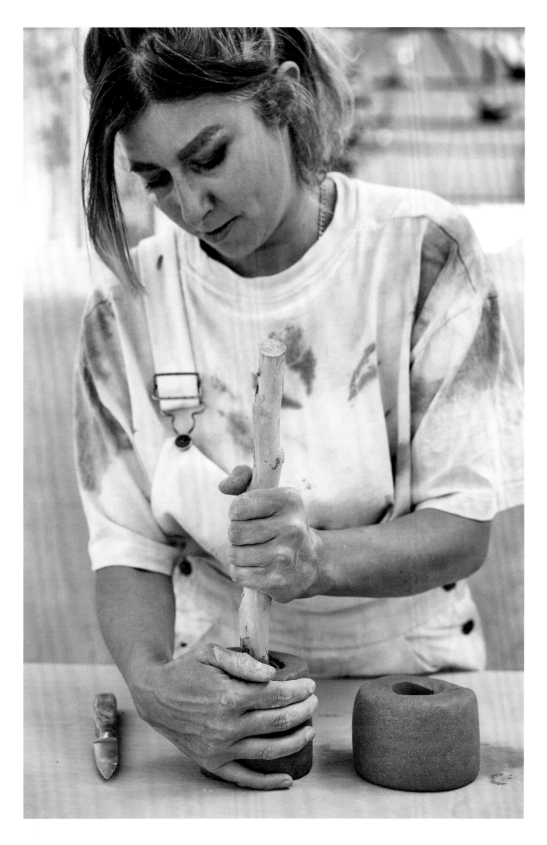

STEP 1:

Pat your two lumps of clay into spheres and roll them on the table to make them into cylinders. Shape one into a short, fat cylinder, and the other into a tall, thin cylinder. Then bash the ends of the cylinders against the table to create the base and top.

STEP 2:

Now take each of your clay cylinders and place them onto a ware board. Plunge the dinner candle into the centre of each, pushing it around one-third of the way into the clay.

STEP 3:

Then with the dinner candle still inside the cylinder, use it to roll the shapes along the board. This is to refine the shape and widen the hole for the candle to go in. Make sure the top and bottom are flat and leave the cylinders on a ware board for an hour or so to go soft leather hard.

TIP: Remember, clay shrinks between 10 and 20 per cent when it's fired, so you need the hole for the candle to be about 15 per cent larger to allow for shrinkage.

STEP 4:

Once soft leather hard, turn the cylinders upside down and use a knife or spoon to carve out a shallow but wide hole, large enough to fit a tea light in, and leave for another couple of hours to go leather hard.

STEP 5:

Once leather hard, use the carving techniques you learnt making the Carved pot (see page 44) to shape your candle holders. I've done a mixture of grating and faceting with the one pictured here. It's up to you whether you carve them both to match or carve a mix of different styles. Remember, the holders need to be heavy enough to stay standing with a tall candle in them, so don't carve away too much clay, leave them chunky.

STEP 6:

Once they are carved you need to refine the holes for the candle. Check the hole for the dinner candle is about 3cm (1¼in) wide and smooth it down with a wooden tool. The hole on the underside for the tea light needs to be around 5cm (2in) wide and 2cm (¾in) deep. Compress and smooth down the top and bottom surfaces as it is important these are both flat for the reversible aspect of the design to work.

STEP 7:

Leave on a ware board to dry for at least 5 days, then fire at cone 06 for 10 hours to bisqueware ready for glazing.

TIP: Big, chunky pieces like this take a long time to dry, so you can leave them on a ware board on the radiator if you want them to dry quicker. If you're not sure if they're bone dry, leave for a few more days. It's better to be safe.

Glaze

I have used a matt white glaze and the pouring method for these pots. Pour your glaze into the candle holes with a jug, leave for 2 seconds, then pour out. Hold the candle holders over a bucket and pour over the glaze. I then use a tool to thin out some parts of the glaze to reveal the bare clay at the edges. Now your candle holders can be fired one last time at cone 8 for 10 hours.

Soap dish

Did you know some dermatologists reckon we shouldn't be using soap, as it kills a load of 'good bacteria' on our skin? Whether these (presumably smelly) experts are right or not, one thing's for certain: I need to put something on my soap dish. I love those things. I've turned my back on the dainty ones though; if you're anything like me you'll have broken a fair few of them in your time. You know, when the soap gunk dries through the drainage holes and fuses the soap, dish and sink together into one claggy bathroom totem and you have to pull so hard to release the soap from its gunk statue that you fling the dish at the opposite wall.

Incidents like this led me to design the SOAP BRICK. It's heavy, it's got ridges and it's got a tray to catch the gunk. It's got everything you could ever ask for in a soap dish, and if you do happen to fling it across a room, it's the wall that's going to be hurting.

STEP 1:

Pat your 1kg (2¼lb) and 1⅔kg (3½lb) hunks of clay into cubes by bashing them against the table, then wrap the smaller one in plastic. Start pinching the 1⅔kg (3½lb) cube into a cuboid-shaped pot. It doesn't need to be an exact cube, just imagine a box missing one side and pinch out roughly that shape, until you have around 1cm- (½in-) walled rough cube pot.

STEP 2:

Now unwrap the 1kg (2¼lb) cube and bash it into a chunky cuboid shape that fits inside the larger cuboid you've just pinched. Use the table to press all six sides of each cuboid flat. Both can be really rough for now, as we just want to get the general shape, which we will refine later. Leave both pieces on a ware board to go leather hard for around 3–5 hours.

STEP 3:

Once leather hard you will be able to carve your big, chunky pinched blocks into more refined shapes. Although for these soap dishes I think the rougher the better – ideally it will look like almost like a rock you found on the beach. Take a cheese grater and use it to grate each face of your cubes flat. Grate over a bowl of water to catch the shavings.

STEP 4:

The 1kg (2¼lb) cube is going to catch the soapy water, so you need to carve a bowl shape into the inside. You want about a 2cm (¾in) thick, smooth bowl shape that's easy to clean. You can use a metal carving tool or a teaspoon to carve out a bit of clay at a time. Once you've carved out enough clay, use a rib to smooth down the inside.

STEP 5:

Make sure that your small cube fits inside the large cube still. Use a knife to refine the inside of the larger cube, then smooth it down with a rib. You might need to go over both cubes again with the grater so that they fit together well. Leave enough of a gap between them to account for shrinkage and warping.

STEP 6:

Now it's time to add ridges to the top of the larger cube so that the soap doesn't get glued to the top every time it dries. Use a spoon or carving tool to remove some clay and make a few ridges. Make the ridges deeper in the middle than at the outside, so the water flows into the centre of each ridge. Then at the centre of each ridge use your knife to create a hole for water to drain through, roughly 10mm × 4mm ($\frac{1}{2}$in × $\frac{1}{8}$in) in size.

TIP: The hole can get closed over when you come to glaze it, so it's important that the hole isn't narrower than 4mm/$\frac{1}{8}$in.

STEP 7:

We also want the ridges to be really smooth, so use your rib or finger to compress the clay. Rubbing your forefinger or the back of a spoon over the clay is, I find, often the best way to get a really smooth finish.

STEP 8:

Go over the whole piece and check you're happy with the finish. It's good to smooth down the edges that are going to touch the surfaces, but I leave the sides quite rough. Scratch your initials on the inside and leave both pieces on a ware board to dry for 3–5 days or until bone dry. Then fire at cone 06 for 10 hours to bisqueware.

Glaze

For this dish I have used a shiny white glaze and the pouring technique. Hold your cube sideways over a bowl and use a jug to pour the glaze over two-thirds of the cube. Leave this to dry, then hold the glazed side of the cube and pour glaze over the other side. Where the glaze is layered or thicker, the colour will be deeper. Now your cubes can be fired one last time at cone 8 for 10 hours.

Set of slab plates

CLAY
– Draycot stoneware
  400g (14oz) lump
  600g (1lb 5oz) lump
  800g (1¾lb) lump

TOOLS
– Kitchen scales
– Rolling pin
– 8mm (⅓in) rolling
  guides
– Rib
– Ware board
– Knife
– Banding wheel or
  newspaper
– Water and sponge

Plates, we've all got them, but can we all make them? Yes, it turns out we can. It's actually really easy to make plates out of slabs of clay, and in this project I'm going to show you how.

An important thing to remember when making plates is to dry them on a flat surface otherwise you end up with a wobbly base, so make sure you have a large flat ware board handy. Another key element I have found with plates is that they need to have a rim to stop oil and other delicious food juices dribbling off. Once you've got these two plate essentials nailed you'll realise it's so easy to make plates you won't be able to stop. And next time I visit, it'll be wall to wall plates.

STEP 1:

Pat your lumps of clay into spheres, then roll them on the table to create cylinders. Take the smallest cylinder and use your rolling pin to bash it flatter on one side, then turn it over and bash it flatter on the other side. When I want my slabs to be more evenly circular, I turn them onto their side and roll them along the desk in between bashing and rolling. This seems to keep the circle more regular. Bash and roll until your slab is between 1 and 2cm (½ and ¾in) thick, then repeat with the other two lumps of clay.

STEP 2:

Now roll and turn each slab until they are 8mm (⅓in) thick – like for the Slab pot and Hump bowl (see pages 32 and 40), roll gently once, flip the slab over and roll again, then turn the slab 180 degrees, roll again, and repeat. This turning and flipping prevents the clay sticking to the table and helps to get an even roll. You can use 8mm (⅓in) dowel as rolling guides if you want, or just go by eye.

STEP 3:

Evenly roll and turn each slab until you have 8mm (⅓in) thick slabs of around 14cm (5½in), 18cm (7in) and 22cm (8½in) diameter each. Use your rib to smooth over any cracks while you are rolling, then give each a final smooth over before you leave them to dry. Leave on a ware board for roughly 1 hour to go soft leather hard.

STEP 4:

Once soft leather hard you can trim the edges to make the plates rounder, or I usually leave the rims uneven for a more unique, natural shape. Use your fingers and thumb to pinch the edges up to create a lip around the plate. The edges should stay up after you've pinched them, if they don't you need to leave them to dry for a bit longer. Go all the way around the edge of each plate pinching and lifting the edges to create a rim. Now leave on a ware board to go leather hard for another hour.

STEP 5:

Once your plates are quite stiff and holding their shape, you can start refining the rims. Put the plate onto a banding wheel or a piece of newspaper and use your rib to smooth down and compress the rim. If you want a rounded rim, gently change the angle of your rib after each rotation, which will round off the edges. If you want a flat rim, trim the edge with a knife, then hold the rib at the same flat angle as you rotate the plates.

STEP 6:

Check the surface of your plates, if they've got cracks or marks anywhere, smooth them over with your rib. Turn the plates over, very gently smooth the bottom and scratch your initials into the clay. Then leave all three on large ware board or flat surface for 2 days to go bone dry and bisque fire at cone 06 for 10 hours.

TIP: Be really gentle when you are smoothing the bottom of your plate; if you lean or press on it too hard you will create tension on the rim and your plate could crack.

Glaze

For these plates I have used a matt cream glaze and the pouring technique. Hold your plate sideways over a bowl and use a jug to pour the glaze over two-thirds of the plate. Leave this to dry, then hold the glazed side of the plate and pour glaze over the other side. Where the glaze is layered or thicker, the colour will be deeper. Wipe any glaze from the bottom with a wet sponge. Now your plates can be fired one last time at cone 8 for 10 hours.

Nest of pinch bowls

CLAY
– Craft crank stoneware
  300g (11oz) lump
  600g (1lb 5oz) lump
  900g (2lb) lump

TOOLS
– Kitchen scales
– Plastic sheet
– Ware board
– Rib
– Knife
– Banding wheel or
  newspaper
– Water and sponge

You'd think with all the pinching I do I'd have really strong hands by now, and yet my BBQ-tong action remains embarrassingly poor. My thumb, or 'the money muscle', as I call it, gets tired and I frequently get hand cramp. And like any top athlete, my greatest fear is somehow irreversibly injuring my pinching thumb. Maybe I could get thumb insurance, like Messi did with his legs?

These days most people tend to use throwing, slip casting and moulding to make anything larger than a cup, and only use the pinching method to make small pots. Pinching a small bowl is no big deal, but pinching a large bowl, some would say, is more trouble than it's worth. Clearly those people have never heard the phrase 'the harder the task, the greater the reward'. The very fact that pinching a large bowl is difficult is, to me, the point of doing it. The resulting bowl is not like any other bowl; it's different and surprising, and that's basically all I've ever wanted from a bowl.

This project is great for taking your pinching skills to the next level. Start with the small bowl and work your way up in size. You'll gradually develop your speed, patience and dexterity, which are the skills you need for pinching.

STEP 1:

Pat your lumps of clay into spheres and wrap the 600g (1lb 5oz) and 900g (2lb) lumps in plastic. Take the 300g (11oz) sphere and push your thumb about two-thirds into the centre. Because this is a bowl and not a pot, rather than pinching out sides and then a base, you are going try to pinch it evenly all over into a shape resembling half a coconut shell. Rotate and pinch evenly all the way around so that the bowl is an even thickness all over. Keep pinching until you have a 1cm- (½in-) thick bowl.

TIP: Because you patted the lump of clay into a sphere, it should naturally want to make a bowl shape as you pinch it. But be aware of the shape as you pinch, so that you don't accidentally pinch it flat into a plate.

STEP 2:

Turn it upside down and place it on a ware board to dry while you pinch the other lumps in exactly the same way. You are aiming to pinch all three bowls into roughly the same shape but each slightly larger, like Russian dolls. Lay each one upside down to dry while you pinch the next one. Don't spend more than 15 minutes on each bowl, otherwise they will dry too hard for the next round of pinching. Pinch each one until it is around 1cm thick and use your rib to smooth down any cracks.

TIP: If you are concerned your bowls might be drying too quickly or it's been longer than 15 minutes, wrap them in plastic, then you can come back to them in your own time. Don't rush, pinching should be relaxing not stressful, and a sheet of plastic will always save the day.

STEP 3:

Once you've pinched all three bowls, go back to the first one. In the time it took you to pinch the others it should have stiffened up a little. Pinch all the way around to make it a bit thinner and more bowl-shaped. You have to be more gentle and slow now that the clay has stiffened, so as not to crack it. Use your rib to smooth down any cracks that appear and to compress the rim from time to time. When you are happy with the shape and thickness, leave the bowl the right way up on the ware board to dry. Move on to the next one and repeat.

STEP 4:

While you are pinching, and before leaving your bowls to go leather hard, check that the medium bowl fits into the large bowl and the small bowl fits into the medium bowl. Pinch the bowls a little more if they don't quite fit. It doesn't need to be as neat as mine as long as they fit inside each other with about a 5mm (¹⁄₅in) gap.

STEP 5:

Now all your bowls are the right way up. Place your hands flat on the rim of the first bowl and push down slightly against your ware board or a flat wooden surface to give the bowl a flat bottom. Repeat this action with the other two bowls and leave to go leather hard.

STEP 6:

Once leather hard it's time to refine the rims and surface. Again, you can choose a flat or curved rim depending on the angle at which you hold your rib. I've trimmed the rim with a knife. Place your bowls one at a time on a banding wheel or on sheets of newspaper and turn underneath your rib or knife. I've used my metal rib held at a right angle to scrape away clay and leave a rough surface.

STEP 7:

Use your rib to smooth down the insides of your bowls. Turn the bowls over and very gently compress the bottoms, then scratch your initials into the clay. Leave all three on a ware board for 2 days to go bone dry, and then bisque fire at cone 06 for 10 hours.

TIP: Be really gentle when you are smoothing the bottom of your bowls; if you lean or press on them too hard you will create tension on the rim and they could crack.

Glaze

For these bowls I have used a matt peach glaze and the pouring technique. Use a jug to pour glaze into the bowl for 2 seconds, then tip it out. Wipe any glaze from the bottom, rim and sides of your bowls with a wet sponge. Now your bowls can be fired one last time at cone 8 for 10 hours.

Pinched coffee jar

CLAY
– Craft crank stoneware
  450g (1lb) lump
  40g (1½oz) lump
  Matching slip

TOOLS
– Kitchen scales
– Knife
– Rib
– Ruler
– Banding wheel or
  newspaper
– Wooden tool
– Ware board
– Fork or serrated-edge
  tool
– Thin wooden sculpting
  tool or lollipop stick
– Water and sponge

People say you can tell a lot about a person from their coffee order. Black Americano? Must be a straight-talking serious type. Prefer a frappa mocha chocco cream thing? You're an indulgent laugh-riot.

I actually think you can tell more about a person based on what they choose to put their coffee in. And I can personally guarantee that coffee does actually taste better from a handmade ceramic jar.

STEP 1:

Pat your 450g (1lb) lump of clay into a cylinder shape. Then plunge your thumb into the centre, two-thirds of the way down and pinch it evenly into a really chunky, wide pinch pot. Compress the rim and smooth down any cracks with your rib.

STEP 2:

Now spend some time pinching it into a coffee jar shape. You're aiming for around 10cm (4in) across by 7cm (2¾in) tall, so keep your ruler handy to see when you are getting close. Try not to pinch any part of the jar too thin in relation to another part of the jar. Very gentle but quick little pinches all the way around are what's needed.

STEP 3:

Once the sides of your jar are getting thinner than 1cm (½in), place on a piece of newspaper or a banding wheel and use your thumb or wooden tool to stretch out the base. I prefer using my thumb because I find it easier to judge the thickness of the base of the jar that way. Again, push down a little at a time so as not to stress the clay.

STEP 4:

Carry on pinching while turning the banding wheel or newspaper, slowly and evenly expanding the pot. Pinch in a circle around the bottom of the wall of the jar, then move your fingers up a little and pinch another circle around the walls and so on until you reach the top of the pot. Compress the rim, then expand the base a little bit more, then start again going up the wall of the jar. Use your rib to smooth down any cracks that appear while you are pinching and to occasionally compress the rim. Repeat. After around 15–20 minutes you should have a jar with roughly 4mm (⅛in) thick sides that's 10cm (4in) round by 7cm (2¾in) tall. Leave it on a ware board for around 2 hours to go leather hard.

STEP 5:

Take the 40g (1½oz) piece of clay and squeeze into a thin sausage, then roll it into a 2cm by 6cm (¾in by 2½in) coil. Leave it drying with your jar.

STEP 6:

Once your jar is leather hard, give it a smooth over with your rib if it needs it, and refine the rim.

STEP 7:

Now you need to attach the handle to the jar using slip and score. Find where you want to attach the end of the handle, make a small mark, then use a fork or serrated-edge tool to scratch and score where the handle will go. Score the end of the handle, too, then apply slip to all scored edges. Now press your handle into the wall of your mug with one hand while supporting it from behind with your other hand. Push gently but firmly, until slip is oozing out and you can feel that the clay bodies have bonded.

STEP 8:

Now take a thin wooden sculpting tool or lollipop stick and blend the handle into the jar. You can make a tiny coil and wrap it around the join to help blend everything together. It's important to use slip and score and pay attention to making sure the join is properly bonded, because you don't want the handle to break off. Go all the way around the join and make sure it is all blended to the jar, the first blend can be a bit rough, then just go around once more to neaten it up.

TIP: Remember to support the clay with your other hand wherever you apply pressure.

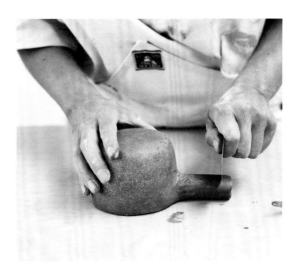

STEP 9:

Make sure you haven't warped the jar or handle too much with the pressure of attaching the handle. I like an irregular shape but it's useful if the coffee jar is still functional. Smooth down the piece with your rib if it needs it, compact and smooth the bottom and leave to dry on a ware board for 2–3 days until bone dry. Bisque fire at cone 06 for 10 hours.

Glaze

For this jar I have used a matt white glaze and the dipping technique. First use a jug to pour glaze into the jar for 2 seconds, then tip it out. Then hold your jar upside down and dip into the glaze about two-thirds of the way in for 2 seconds and lift out. Wipe any glaze from the bottom with a wet sponge. Now your jar can be fired one last time at cone 8 for 10 hours.

Large platter

CLAY

– Draycot stoneware
  2kg (4½lb) lump
  Black slip

TOOLS

– Kitchen scales
– Rolling pin
– Rolling guides
– Large ware board
  (over 40 × 40cm)
– Wooden tool
– Rib
– Soft-bristled paintbrush
– Metal rib
– Water and sponge

Dinner parties just don't cut the mustard unless you bring out a huge platter of spiced lamb, drizzled with black garlic foam and turmeric yogurt, or so Yotam Ottolenghi would have us believe. So if you're going to go to the trouble of grinding four hundred ingredients into a fine paste and roasting a lamb haunch for 20 hours to impress your friends, you'd better have an amazing ceramic platter to serve them on.

This is made in the same way that we made the slab plates, just on a much bigger scale. On this large platter, however, we are going to use our slip decorating skills to paint a picture on it to make it really special.

STEP 1:

Take your 2kg (4½lb) lump of clay and pat it into a large sphere. Then roll the sphere on the desk to make it cylindrical. Put it on the work bench and use your rolling pin to bash it flatter on one side, then flip it over and bash it flatter on the other side. Pick it up and roll it on its side, place it flat and bash it on both sides again. Bash, flip, roll and turn the sphere until you have a big chunky disc, about 2–3cm (¾–1¼in) thick and 20cm (8in) wide.

STEP 2:

Now place the disk onto your large ware board and use rolling guides to roll it into a big circle about 8mm (⅓in) thick by 40cm (16in) wide. Keep turning and flipping as you roll so that the slab doesn't stick to the ware board. Use your rib to smooth the surface and edges as you roll.

TIP: This is a large slab to roll out, so take your time, otherwise the clay will be under too much stress and could crack.

STEP 3:

Once you have rolled it out to approximately 8mm (⅓in) thick, smooth down the rim and both sides with your rib. Then leave on the large ware board to firm up to soft leather hard for about 1 hour, but don't let it go fully leather hard.

TIP: Work on the platter on the ware board from this point on. As it is a large flat piece it's better not to move or lift it without support. If you do need to lift it off the board, use both hands with spread fingers.

STEP 4:

Now the slab has firmed up, start pinching the rim up. I usually go about 4cm (1½in) inward from the rim and pinch up from there. Go all the way round the platter a couple of times, then leave to go leather hard for another hour or so.

STEP 5:

Smooth down the surface of the platter in gentle sweeping strokes with your rib. Smooth down the areas where you pinched up the sides and compress the rim and refine it to your liking. I've gone round the rim with the rib a few times, changing the angle with each rotation to create a rounded-off rim.

STEP 6:

Mix up your black slip and use a soft-bristled brush to draw a picture on your platter. I've done a very simple female form on mine, but you could do a face or just some swooshes with the brush to make an abstract pattern. Leave the first layer to dry, then apply another layer.

TIP: If you make any mistakes or drips with the slip, wait for them to dry, then scrape off with the straight edge of a metal rib. You could also draw out your motif on a piece of paper in pencil then practise your drawing in slip on the paper first.

STEP 7:

Once the slip is completely dry, check the base of your platter – if there are any cracks or marks, smooth them over with your rib. Scratch your initials into the clay on the base, then leave on a ware board for 2–3 days to go bone dry. Bisque fire at cone 06 for 10 hours.

TIP: Be really gentle when you are smoothing the bottom of your platter; if you lean or press on it too hard you will create tension on the rim and your plate could crack.

Glaze

For this platter I have used a transparent glaze and the dipping method. Apply wax resist to the bottom of the platter, wait for it to dry and then using tongs dip the whole platter into the glaze and straight out again. Wipe any glaze from the bottom with a wet sponge and now your platter can be fired one last time at cone 8 for 10 hours.

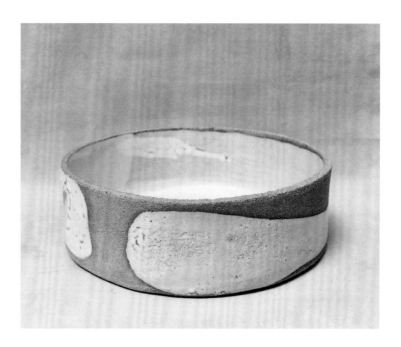

Deep dish

CLAY
– Craft crank stoneware
  1⅔kg (3½lb) lump
  2 × 1.2kg (2¾lb) lumps
  150g (5oz) lump
  Matching slip

TOOLS
– Kitchen scales
– Rolling pin
– Ruler
– 1cm (½in) rolling guides
– Rib
– 2 × large ware boards
– Newspaper
– Knife
– Paintbrush
– Wooden tools
– Metal tool
– Curved tool or teaspoon
– Water and sponge

Hands up if you like parties! You can't see me, but I just threw both arms in the air! Massive deep dishes are brilliant for serving up big, delicious sharing food at parties. This dish can easily hold enough nosh to keep your friends and family, or a Great Dane, full for a week. But don't worry if feeding everyone and their dog isn't your bag, this dish also functions as a charming fruit bowl.

It's essentially a big old slab pot. So exactly the same principles apply here as with your small slab pot, except it's larger and scarier to make. You need to allow more drying time, more slip and more space to make it, otherwise you might end up as I did the first time I attempted one of these behemoths and having a mini meltdown halfway through.

STEP 1:

Pat your 1⅔kg (3½lb) hunk of clay into a sphere. Use your rolling pin to bash, turn and roll it out into a 30cm (12in) wide circular slab about 1cm (½in) thick. Then pat the two 1.2kg (2¾lb) hunks into rectangles and roll out each into 10cm × 48cm × 1cm (4in × 19in × ½in) thick slabs using 1cm (½in) pieces of dowel, or go by eye. Remember to turn and flip the clay for an even roll. Smooth down all sides of the clay with a rib and leave to dry on ware boards for an hour or so until soft leather hard.

TIP: If you're not confident rolling out accurate slabs, add half of the stated amount of clay to your existing lump and roll out bigger slabs that you can trim to size.

STEP 2:

Once your slabs are soft leather hard you need to prep them for building. Place the circular slab onto a piece of newspaper on a large ware board. Score the top edge of your circular slab about 1cm (½in) in all the way around.

TIP: For this dish we are attaching the walls to the top of the base rather than the sides of the base as this offers more support for a wide-based piece. It also means you don't have to turn the platter over when blending, which can lead to collapsing and warping.

STEP 3:

Use your knife to cut the short edges of each rectangle slab at a 45-degree angle. Then score the bottom and side edges of both rectangular slabs. Place your rectangular slabs onto a couple of sheets of newspaper each and apply the slip to all the scored edges relatively swiftly with a brush. You don't need to be neat and you don't want the slip to dry before you start to build, so use a big brush and daub it on nice and thick.

STEP 4:

Time to build.

TIP: It's a big piece so leave yourself plenty of time, it will take longer than you think to blend it all together. And this where it can all go wrong, especially if you haven't let the clay go leather hard, so take it slowly.

Gently lift one of your rectangle slabs by lifting the newspaper at each end. The newspaper will support the whole slab and allow you to bend it to the curve of the platter. Place the scored edge of the wall slab along the scored edge of the base slab and adjust it so the scored edges meet up all the way around. Apply a tiny bit of pressure around the top with your wooden tool until the wall stays in place. Then repeat this on the other side of the base with the other wall slab. Squeeze the two joins of the wall slabs together with your fingers and wooden tool, and breathe – that's the hard bit done.

STEP 5:

Take a large ware board and place it on top of the walls of your platter (like a big ice-cream sandwich) and using both hands gently press down until you see the slip oozing from the base and the clay bodies bonding.

STEP 6:

For extra support I roll out coils to blend into the inside of the base join. So grab the 150g (5oz) lump of clay, split it in two and roll out two thin coils that roughly make 95cm (37in) in length combined, then push these into the join on the inside of the pot. Blend this with the curved edge of a wooden tool all the way around.

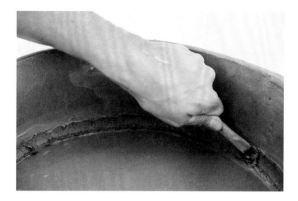

STEP 7:

Blend together all the joins using a wooden tool. Start at the base and use your tool to push and blend the clay upward from the bottom, turning the ware board so you work all the way around the dish. Then move onto the two joins on the walls of the dish and blend these with your wooden tool.

STEP 8:

Now use a rib to smooth down the entire dish, paying special attention to the areas with all your blending. Use a curved tool, like a lollipop stick or a teaspoon, to smooth down the blending on the inside.

STEP 9:

Look all over your piece and check you are happy with the finish. For the dish pictured I've used the edge of a metal tool to scrape away some of the surface of the clay from the walls to create some rough edges. Compress and refine the rim; I've trimmed the rim on the pot pictured flat with a knife. Scratch your initials into the bottom and leave to go bone dry for 2–3 days, then fire at cone 06 for 10 hours.

Glaze

For this dish I have used a matt white glaze and the pouring technique. First fill a jug and pour a large amount of glaze into the dish; quickly lift it up and swirl it around, then tip it out. Wait for this to dry, then hold your dish sideways over a bucket and use a jug to pour the glaze over two-thirds of it. Leave this to dry, then hold the dish sideways on the glazed side of the bowl and pour more glaze over the other side. Where the glaze is layered or thicker, the colour will be deeper. Wipe any glaze from the bottom with a wet sponge. Now your dish can be fired one last time at cone 8 for 10 hours.

Totem

CLAY
– Craft crank
  4 × 400g (14oz) lumps
  600g (1lb 5oz) lump
  Black slip

TOOLS
– Kitchen scales
– Bamboo cane
– Ware board
– Carving tools
– Paintbrush
– Rib
– Knife
– Water and sponge

I actually pinched this idea from Channel 4's *The Great Pottery Throw Down*. They made a much larger version, whereas I've gone for a table-top-size totem. While I hope most of the projects in this book are accessible, it occurred to me that this project in particular is brilliantly accessible. You can apply loads of techniques or almost no techniques and still end up with something that looks really cool. It's like pottery by numbers. All you need is lumps of clay with holes through the middle and a stick to put them on. I found an old bamboo cane in the garden and trimmed it down to size.

STEP 1:

Pat your 400g (14oz) lumps of clay into two spheres and two cubes. Take your stick and plunge it all the way through the middle of each piece and out the other side. Wiggle the stick around inside each block of clay to make a gap 1cm (½in) bigger than the stick. Leave to dry on a ware board for 4–6 hours or until leather hard.

STEP 2:

Pat your 600g (1lb 5oz) lump into a sphere or cube – this is going to be the base of your totem, so make it wider than the others. Use the stick to make a hole in the centre but don't go all the way through the clay this time. Leave 2cm (¾in) of clay at the base. Wiggle the stick around a bit to enlarge the hole, then leave on a ware board to go leather hard with the others.

STEP 3:

Once leather hard, use your carving tools to carve different shapes out of each piece of clay. It's up to you what shapes you make using the techniques you learned in the carving projects. I've done large, simple shapes and symbols like you might see on ancient totems.

STEP 4:

Now use your brush to paint the carved out shapes with black slip. Leave the slip to dry, then paint on another layer of slip and leave that to dry for an hour. When you return to your shapes check that they are dry all over, use a metal rib to scrape away any excess slip and refine the shape.

STEP 5:

Check over the finish and smooth the top and bottom of each shape, paying particular attention to the top and bottom of the pieces. It's important that they are flat so that they stack well.

STEP 6:

Once you've decorated your shapes to your liking, check they all fit onto your stick, accounting for 20 per cent shrinkage when firing. Check over the finish and smooth the top and bottom of each shape, paying particular attention to the bottom of the base piece, making sure it is flat and smooth.

STEP 7:

Scratch your initials into the bottom and leave to go bone dry for 3–5 days, then fire at cone 06 for 10 hours.

Glaze

I have painted shiny black glaze over the slipped parts of the totem to strengthen the colour. Paint a layer carefully over the slip, let it dry and then paint another layer. Then fire one last time at cone 8 for 10 hours.

PROJECTS

HARD

Coiled vase

CLAY
– Craft crank stoneware
  500g (1lb 2oz) lump
  20 × 150g (5oz) lumps
  Matching slip

TOOLS
– Kitchen scales
– Ruler
– Rib
– Ware board
– Wooden tool
– Plastic sheet
– Water spray bottle
– Spatula
– Water and sponge

So you've made a mini coil vase and that was simple enough, right? Now it's time to flex your coiling muscles and make a ruddy huge one. Don't be afraid, I'm here to hold your hands – your shaking, clay-covered hands…

The beauty of coiling is that it's good for wrapping up in plastic and coming back to later, so don't stress yourself out rushing this piece, take your time and enjoy the making. If you have such a good time you finish it in one day, great! If not, wrap it in plastic with a damp sponge (this keeps it humid) and come back to it later. A bit like knitting, you can have this project waiting for you in the corner for when your creative juices start flowing.

STEP 1:

Pat the 500g (1lb 2oz) lump of clay into a sphere, then pinch it into a 1cm (½in) thick by 10cm (4in) wide bowl to make a base. Give it a once-over with your rib, then gently press it down onto a ware board to give it a flat bottom. Leave to dry a little while you roll out a coil. Squeeze a 120g (4oz) chunk of clay into a sausage, then roll out a coil to about 1cm (½in) wide by 32cm (12½in) long. Place the coil around the rim of the base and use a wooden tool to blend the coil to the base.

TIP: Remember to blend on the inside and outside of the coil.

STEP 2:

For this coil vase I'm going to go in and out twice to create two bulges. To achieve the bulges, the first five coils I roll get heavier by 20g (¾oz) of clay and wider by 4cm (1½in) each time and I fix them slightly to the outside of the top of last coil. Then I start to go back in by reducing the weight and length of coil by 20g (¾oz) and 4cm (1½in) each time. (120g, 140g, 160g, 180g, 200g / 4oz, 4¾oz, 5½oz, 6¼oz, 7oz; and 32cm, 36cm, 40cm, 44cm, 48cm/ 12½in, 14in, 15½in, 17in, 18½in)

TIP: If you need to stop for more than 20 minutes, wrap the entire piece in plastic to keep it moist until you return. Keep a water spray bottle handy to spritz it if parts of the vase are drying out too quickly. And remember to seal the bag of clay each time you grab a hunk for a coil.

STEP 3:

Repeat step 2 once more or until you have reached the height and shape you're after. You can stop here, refine the rim and surface of your vase and let it go bone dry, or if you want to add some decorative coils to your vase follow the next few steps.

STEP 4:

Roll out four chunky coils using 250g (9oz) lumps of clay. Make them roughly 2cm (¾in) wide by 22cm (8½in) long. Then wet them a little and bend them into circles, squeezing the ends together until you feel the clay bond and blend. (You don't need slip and score here because the clay will still be quite wet.) Use your rib to smooth over any cracks and leave them to dry for around 30 minutes.

STEP 5:

Now work out where you want to place your hoops on your vase. It's important that the weight is distributed evenly, so bear this in mind when positioning them. If you aren't sure, just copy mine. The vase is likely to need to contain tall stems, so it is already going to be a bit top-heavy and it would be a shame to do all this work and end up with a vase that falls over.

STEP 6:

Mark the positions chosen for your hoops, then slip and score them to the walls of your vase. You can use really thin coils to reinforce the join.

STEP 7:

Go over the hoops and the whole vase with your spatula and rib until you are happy with the finish. Use a slightly damp sponge to wipe down if needed. I've scraped away the top layer of clay to achieve a more rustic finish on the vase but left the hoops smooth as a contrast.

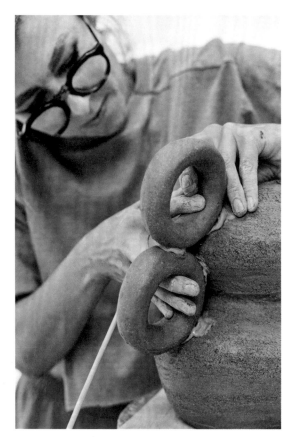

STEP 8:

Carefully compress and smooth down the base and the rim of your vase with a rib and scratch your initials into the bottom. Leave to go bone dry for 3–5 days and fire at cone 06 for 10 hours to bisqueware.

Glaze

For this vase I have left the body unglazed and dipped the rings in a matt black glaze. First paint wax resist on the vase around the rings, enough so that you can dip the rings without getting glaze on the vase body. Fill a jug to pour a large amount of glaze into the vase, then tip it out while rotating the vase in your hand to make sure all of the inside is covered. Wait for this to dry, then hold your vase sideways over a bucket of glaze and dip the rings all the way into the glaze for 2 seconds, then lift out. Wipe any glaze from the body and the bottom of the vase with a wet sponge. Now your vase can be fired one last time at cone 8 for 10 hours.

Face sculpture

CLAY
– Craft crank stoneware
  2 × 800g (1¾lb) lumps
  1 × 600g (1lb 5oz) lump
  Matching slip

TOOLS
– Kitchen scales
– Rolling guides
– Rolling pin
– Ruler
– Metal rib
– Ware board
– Sculpting knife
– Teaspoon
– Soft-bristled paintbrush
– Wooden tool

Who doesn't want to encapsulate a likeness of their own face in permanent ceramic form for future people to find and blame the destruction of the planet on? Me, that's who, so I've captured my friend Holly instead. Holly is like Mary Poppins; practically perfect in every way. She's feminine, smart, funny, generous, older in spirit than her years and a perfectionist. Here I've captured her spirit in an abstract sculpture of her face. Once she grew a unibrow, as if to prove she has flaws, so I thought I'd throw that in too. I'm not sure I captured her soul, to be honest, but this sculpture, like its muse, makes me happy every time I see it.

To me, abstract art is more engaging than ultra-realistic art. That's not to say that being able to capture a realistic likeness isn't an awe-inspiring skill, but in trying capture true accuracy you can sometimes lose what I look for in art: playfulness, creativity, originality and expression. A piece that has an energy about it will always bring me joy. This type of sculpture is perfect for beginners to express their creativity without the restrictions of accuracy. In this project I want you to try to capture a friend or family member. Ask yourself; who is this person, what do they stand for and how can I convey their vibe in an abstract sculpture of their face?

STEP 1:

Pat one 800g (1¾lb) lump of clay into a sphere and bash and roll into a slab. Use rolling guides or dowel to roll it out to about 22cm (8½in) circle about 2cm (¾in) thick. Then roll out another slab with the 600g (1lb 5oz) lump of clay, any shape about 12mm (½in) thick. (Turn, flip and roll!) Now use the table or a wooden surface to slam the other 800g (1¾lb) hunk of clay into a rectangular cuboid block. Smooth them all down with a rib and leave for an hour or so to go leather hard.

STEP 2:

Now take your 22cm (8½in) circular slab and decide what shape you want it to be. You can leave it flat (which is much easier and still looks great, in which case skip this step and step 6) or you can give it a 3D feel. Holly has quite a big, round head so I'm only going to trim it a little, leaving it quite round. She has an amazing profile, which I'm going to capture by giving the sculpture a profile. She also has a tiny nose, so I'm going to cut that out of the profile to represent this. Slice through the clay at a 45-degree angle against a straight edge. I'm going to make this one neater than my normal sculptures, because she's a perfectionist. Flip the largest piece of the slab over; this will allow you to re-attach the smaller piece at an angle later, creating a 3D sculpture. I've also cut out a triangle from the profile to represent Holly's nose.

STEP 3:

Now I'm going to use the 600g (1lb 5oz) slab to cut shapes out that will be Holly's lips and eyebrows and I've used thin coils and balls for the eyes and eyelashes. We are going for energy not reality, so keep this in mind as you cut out your shapes.

STEP 4:

Hollow out the back of your block a little, around 2½cm × 2½cm (1in × 1in) so that it dries quicker and doesn't crack inside the kiln. This is going to be the mount for your sculpture. With a teaspoon, carve a 1cm (½in) curved dip in the top of your block that roughly matches the bottom of your sculpture.

STEP 5:

Now lay these shapes where you want them on your face slab or slabs and mark gently with a knife. Then use slip and score to carefully press them into position. I'm not going to blend here because I like the sharp edges. Remember not to fix any details to the part of the face that is going to be fixed into the 1cm (½in) hole in your mounting block.

STEP 6:

If you decided to make your sculpture 3D, slip and score the edges of your face slab you cut earlier and squeeze the edges together. You can use a straight edge like a ruler or piece of dowel to support the straight edge as you bond the pieces together. Blend and smooth the join over with your rib.

STEP 7:

Mount your face into the block by slipping and scoring all edges that are going to touch and gently pressing into place.

STEP 8:

Smooth down the base and scratch on your initials. Leave to dry for a week (the block is going to need a lot of time to dry out completely) then fire at cone 06 for 10 hours.

Glaze

For this sculpture I've painted glaze onto the features and left the rest raw clay. Use a soft-bristled brush to paint red glaze onto the lips and black onto the unibrow. Wipe any glaze from the bottom with a wet sponge, then your sculpture can be fired one last time at cone 8 for 10 hours.

Candlesticks

CLAY

– Craft crank stoneware
  2 × 2kg (4½lb) lumps
  2 × 1kg (2¼lb) lumps

TOOLS

– Kitchen scales
– Rolling pin (ideally
  3cm/1¼in diameter)
– Ruler
– Ware board
– Plastic sheet
– Sculpting knife
– Wooden tool
– Metal rib
– Water and sponge

Tall candlesticks are atmospheric and decadent and I find them irresistible, especially at bath time. Discounting weirdly shaped soap dishes, this is my most-made item (it's wall to wall candlesticks and soap dishes in my bathroom), and after a lot of experimentation this design probably is my favourite. They look to me like objects that could have been excavated from some ancient 'Bell Beaker' settlement (a European archaeological culture famous for inventing, yes, the beaker).

These candlesticks are a complicated make, but they look great, and in this project you will develop lots of carving and sculpting skills. Sculpting in clay is all about drying times. You need to make the basic shape first, then have the patience to let it dry hard enough to be worked on but not so hard that it cracks and falls apart. If you don't get it right the first time, don't be disheartened, as it takes practice. You have to have failures when you are making, failing is learning. Not to mention that drying times vary depending on the clay you're using, the temperature and the humidity. Once you've mastered these skills there is no limit to the different shapes of candlesticks you can try using this method.

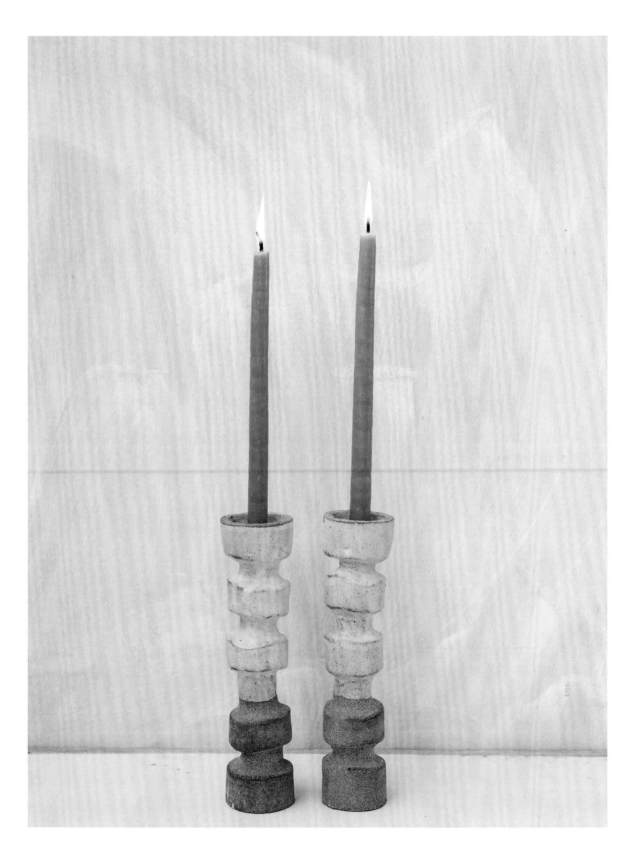

STEP 1:

Take one of your 1kg (2¼lb) lumps of clay, pat the clay into an oval sphere, then squeeze it into an even 'sausage' shape nice and thick, around 4cm (1½in). Roll this with your hands on a flat surface until it is roughly 3cm (1¼in) thick and 20cm (8in) long. This will make the shaft of your candlesticks. Do this twice, then leave them on your ware board to dry for a couple of hours or until leather hard.

STEP 2:

Bash one of the 2kg (4½lb) lumps of clay, pat into a sphere, then bash the sides against the table to create a rough cube. Use your rolling pin to bash the cube flatter, turning and flipping the clay so that you work it evenly. Roll it into a 13cm × 20cm × 2cm (5in × 8in × ¾in) slab.

STEP 3:

Now take your rolling pin and roll this slab landscape around the rolling pin to create a cylinder. The inside of your cylinder should be no bigger than 3cm (1¼in) diameter. Repeat this process with the other 2kg (4½lb) of clay. Stand the two cylinders on some plastic sheet and leave to go soft leather hard, then use your sculpting knife to cut the cylinder into five 4cm (1½in) wide rings.

STEP 4:

Slide five rings onto each of your shafts, taking care not to damage or bend the clay shaft. You need to have two rings at either end (only half on the shaft) and three spaced out evenly in the middle. Use your fingers to squish the rings around the shaft, then use the wooden tool to blend the rings to the shaft, applying enough pressure to seal the edges of each ring but not bend the shaft. Blend the shaft to the inside of the top and bottom rings, leaving a hole for a candle.

STEP 5:

Give everything a rough smooth over with your wooden tool, then wrap the ends in a little plastic. Make sure the sticks are straight, then leave them to dry on their side for around 6 hours. The plastic at either end stops the ends drying out while the chunkier centre of the sticks has a chance to stiffen up so that it doesn't bend while you are sculpting and refining the shape.

STEP 6:

Once dry enough to hold their shape, you need to work on either end of the candlestick first. At the top end, use your wooden tool to create a space big enough for a tealight – around 4½–5cm (approx. 2in) diameter, 2cm (¾in) deep. Then neaten up the bottom with the same tool and push the base into the table and rotate to make sure it is flat on the bottom and the candlestick stands up straight.

STEP 7:

Now use your wooden tool and rib to carve and sculpt the candlesticks into the shape you want. I like to smooth it all down with the wooden tool first so you can't see any joins, then carve bits of clay away using my metal rib to make the surface rough and the shape more irregular.

STEP 8:

Next make sure the hole in the top of your sticks is wide and deep enough to hold a dinner candle. I use a wooden tool 5mm wider than a dinner candle and rotate it inside the hole to account for shrinkage. Leave the sticks to dry for 5 days before firing at cone 06 for 10 hours.

Glaze

For these candlesticks I have used a satin cream glaze and the dipping technique. Use a jug to pour the glaze into the candle hole, swirl it around to get full coverage with the glaze and pour it back out. Then dip the candle two-thirds of the way into the glaze, hold for 4 seconds and lift out. Wipe any glaze from the bottom with a wet sponge. Now your candlesticks can be fired one last time at cone 8 for 10 hours.

Goddess vase

Certainty is alluring, comforting even, but it is an illusion. I am distrustful of anyone who is 'certain'. Many people have been certain about the 'ideal' female form throughout history, but since the surprisingly egalitarian ancient Minoans, what represents 'ideal' has been largely dictated by men. Today some women are taking back ownership over how their bodies are represented through self-expression.

I personally think seeing each others' wobbly bits is a great way to combat shame and boost confidence. As a fan of nudity, I also have a strong appreciation for our largest bodily organ, our skin. I like flesh and a lot of it. I want to see melanin-rich skin, fair skin and everything outside and in between. I want to see big bodies, small bodies and irregular bodies. I genuinely hated my body for failing me for a long time, but looking at loads of buttocks, breasts, necks, penises, vulvas, stomachs and backs to make my Goddess Vases helped me fall in love with my body again, however 'broken' it may be. Feel free to make your Goddess Vase with a penis, or breasts and a penis – or neither. Don't let society dictate what you think is beautiful. However you identify, this vase is a celebration of all the exquisite and varied miracles that are our bodies.

STEP 1:

Take your 600g (1lb 5oz) lump of clay and pat it into a sphere, then use your thumb and index finger to squeeze it in the middle to create a sort of hourglass shape.

STEP 2:

Use your rolling pin to bash this shape flat against your bench evenly on both sides until it is around 2cm (¾in) thick and then roll it out to 1cm (½in) thick. This will be the bottom of your vase. Leave it to dry on a ware board for 30 minutes while you prep the rest of the clay.

STEP 3:

Now bash your 400g (14oz) lumps of clay into squares and flatten evenly with your rolling pin. Roll them out into roughly rectangular-shaped 1cm (½in) slabs. Leave them to stiffen up for around 30 minutes, then wrap them in plastic.

TIP: If you want particularly big buttocks or breasts on your vase, use a couple of 800g (1¾lb) lumps of clay. Roll out a couple of 2cm (¾in) thick slabs instead of 1cm (½in) so you have plenty of clay to work with.

STEP 4:

Now you're going to attach the slabs that will become the thighs, vulva (or penis) and buttocks of your vase. Daub a little water around the top edge of the base of your vase, then take one of your prepared slabs and place it on the base, shaping it to the edge. It should cover roughly half of the base. Press down until you feel it bond, then use your wooden tool to drag clay from the base upward, and blend the two slabs together. Now repeat this with another slab on the other side of your base and blend all the edges of the slabs together.

STEP 5:

I use pinching here to shape the slabs. You can think of the buttocks as pinch bowls and pinch out two little or big bowls. I leave a little bit of space underneath the buttocks for the tops of the thighs. Then pinch out the front and backs of the thighs and the vulva.

TIP: Don't feel like this vase has to be true to life, some of the best goddess vases I've made are very abstract, primitive or exaggerated.

STEP 6:

Use your wooden tool to press into the clay and accentuate the creases between the thighs, vulva and buttocks. You can also use your wooden tool from the inside to expand the clay outward. Use your rib to smooth down any cracks and be careful not to pinch the clay too thin.

STEP 7:

Take another two slabs and squeeze them onto the top of the buttocks and thighs you've just created. Use your wooden tool to blend them all together. These pieces are the small of the back and the stomach. Again, feel free to use extra clay to make a big belly or a chubby back or less clay to make a narrow waist. Then pinch in or out the shape you are after. Use your wooden tool for shaping and blending and your rib to smooth down any cracks.

TIP: If you need more clay for an area, just tear some off one of your prepped slabs and add or blend it to the vase where needed. The more clay you add the more weight the vase has to support. I actually really like the sagging that can occur on this make, but you might want to support your vase with a chunk of clay or let it dry a bit if it's starting to collapse.

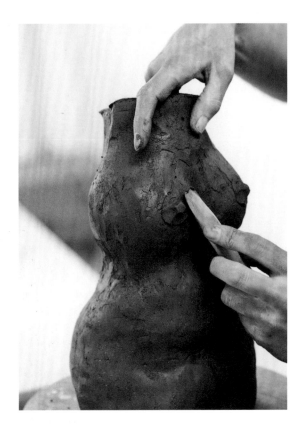

STEP 8:

Repeat step 7 for the upper back and breasts. Again, use a thicker slab if you are planning to pinch large breasts. I put the nipples on the breasts later, so don't worry about those for now. With breasts it's good to remember that they are always further apart than you think they are going to be. Push-up bras have them facing forward and often your nipples are looking in different directions. Then you can add more clay to narrow back in for the neck of the vase.

STEP 9:

To add nipples to your vase, pinch a little clay from one of your slabs and roll it into two balls. Push these onto the breasts and press down gently. Then use a rib to pull the sides of the balls down in about five motions and you'll find this creates what looks a bit like areola. You can also add pubic hair at this point, and other details you like. Go over the whole vase with your rib, smoothing over and adding texture. Refine the rim and smooth down the bottom.

STEP 10:

Use a soft-bristled brush to apply your contrasting slip. I tend to apply this fairly freely, with big sweeping brushstrokes. Leave the first layer to dry for roughly 30 minutes, then apply a second layer. Then scratch your initials into the bottom and leave on a ware board to dry for 3–5 days until bone dry. Fire at cone 06 for 10 hours.

Glaze

For the goddess I have used a shiny black to glaze only the inside of the vase and the nipples and vulva. Use a jug to pour the glaze into the vase, rotate it as you pour it out to get full coverage. Then paint a couple of layers of the glaze onto the nipples and vulva with a brush. Wipe any glaze from the bottom with a wet sponge, then your goddess can be fired one last time at cone 8 for 10 hours.

Sculptural bookends

CLAY
– Draycot stoneware
  2 × 800g (1¾lb) lumps
  4 × 1kg (2¼lb) lumps
  2 × 1.2kg (2¾lb) lumps
  Matching slip

TOOLS
– Kitchen scales
– Rolling pin
– Ware board
– Grater
– Metal rib
– Knife
– Sculpting knife
– Water and sponge

Books are amazing. The source of human knowledge. Beautiful, fascinating, terrifying, romantic, significant and crucial. It's an indisputable fact that books are good for the soul. But what they aren't good for is 'standing up by themselves'. That's where bookends come in.

In this project you will learn how to make a pair of abstract sculptural bookends. When it comes to bookends the only really important thing is that they look good and they are heavy – which is such a broad brief, if you think about it. So try these or use this as a guide, combined with the other skills you've learned so far, to go wild. GO ON, for once in your life, Linda, let your goddamn hair down.

STEP 1:

Bash all your lumps of clay against the table to make rough cube shapes. Then take your rolling pin and plunge it through the centre of each cube, stopping about 3cm (1¼in) from the bottom.

STEP 2:

Take one of your cubes and put the rolling pin back inside it. Use the rolling pin as a handle to bash the lump of clay into an irregular shape – it should still be roughly a cube shape overall but with a few more angles. Repeat with all eight cubes and leave on a ware board to dry for 2–3 hours or until soft leather hard.

STEP 3:

Once soft leather hard, use your grater to neaten up the sides you created on your cubes earlier. Grate over a bowl of water to catch the shavings and remove enough clay from each side to give a nice sharp angle. The shape of the cubes doesn't matter too much, except on the 1.2kg (2¾lb) cubes. At least two sides of these heavier cubes need to be a right angle, because they are going to buttress up against the shelf and the books. So make sure you take this into account when you are grating.

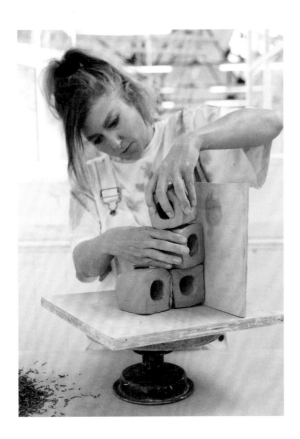

STEP 4:

Now it's time to construct your sculptural bookends. They can be arranged quite randomly, as long as the heaviest cube is at the bottom and the entire piece has a right angle on one side. You also want to place the cubes so that the hollow sides are at the back. Have a little play around with the arrangement by planning it out on the desk first. Once you are happy, make marks where the cubes are going to join. Prop a ware board up to make sure the opposite side of each bookend is at a right angle.

STEP 5:

Build your sculptural bookends by slipping and scoring all the joining edges together. You don't need to do any blending, so make sure you squeeze the clay together and feel it properly bond. Use your wooden tool on the inside of the holes to apply pressure and make sure the clay is bonded, supporting it from behind with your fingers. Leave for 30 minutes to stiffen.

STEP 6:

Once the structure has stiffened use the grater to make sure the sides that buttress against the books and shelf are at a right angle. Then level off and neaten up the back of the bookends and hollow out the back a little more. Use your metal rib and wooden tool on the front of the bookends to scrape away the grating marks and refine the surface and shape

STEP 7:

Check over the finish of your bookends, wipe away any excess slip and neaten up the edges with a metal rib. Smooth down the bottom and scratch in your initials. Leave to dry on a ware board for a week (the blocks are going to need a lot of time to dry out completely), then fire at cone 06 for 10 hours.

Glaze

For these bookends I have used a transparent glaze and the dipping technique on one bookend and left the other raw clay. Simply hold the bookend from the back with your fingers in the holes and dip the front into the bucket of glaze for 2 seconds, then lift out. Wipe any excess glaze from the sides and bottom with a wet sponge, then your bookends can be fired one last time at cone 8 for 10 hours.

Pedestal bowl

CLAY
– Volcan medium stoneware
  2 × 1kg (2¼lb) lumps
  Matching slip

TOOLS
– Kitchen scales
– Rolling pin
– Rolling guides
– Ruler
– Large ware board
– Large bowl
– Plastic sheet
– Newspaper
– Rib
– Knife
– Water and sponge

Putting a bowl on a pedestal lifts it to new heights literally, but also aesthetically. And in a bid to feel like I'm living in a Greek play, I have lots of bowls on pedestals. Obviously they come in really handy for all the elegant banquets I host, and the rest of the time they make pretentious homes for keys, jewellery and fruit.

STEP 1:

Pat one of the 1kg (2¼lb) lumps of clay into a sphere. Then use your rolling pin to bash, flip and roll it out into a 30cm (12in) diameter circular slab about 8mm (⅓in) thick. Bash the other 1kg (2¼lb) of clay on the table into a square, then bash, flip and roll it into a 40cm × 10cm (16in × 4in) rectangle slab about 1cm (½in) thick. Leave the slabs to stiffen for 30 minutes on a ware board.

STEP 2:

In the meantime, line your chosen bowl with a layer of plastic, then a layer of newspaper, then take the large circular slab and drape it over the bowl. Pat it down gently until it has taken on the shape of your hump mould. Use your rib to gently smooth down the outside of your bowl around the mould.

STEP 3:

Take the rectangular slab and cut a 45-degree angle along the short ends like you did for your first slab pot, then slip and score the edges. Stand it on its side and shape into a cylinder. Squeeze the edges together until the slip oozes out, and blend using your wooden tool. Smooth it down using your rib. Leave your cylinder and bowl drying for 1–2 hours or until soft leather hard.

STEP 4:

Once soft leather hard you can join the stand and bowl together. First mark out where the join is going to be. With the bowl still upturned on its mould, sit the stand on top and make sure it is placed evenly in the centre. Take your knife and mark the bottom of your bowl where the stand will join to it.

STEP 5:

Roll out two 40cm (16in) coils and put to one side to dry a little. Now score the edge of the stand that you will join to the bowl and score the bottom of the bowl where you marked it and daub both with slip. Place the freshly slipped stand onto the bowl. Take a ware board and place it on top of both and carefully press down until you can see all the slip oozing out.

STEP 6:

Take one of the coils and press it into the inside of the base to reinforce the join. Then press the other coil into the stand and bowl to reinforce the bond from the outside. Blend both coils in with your wooden tool and thoroughly smooth down. Leave to dry for another 30 minutes or until fully leather hard.

STEP 7:

Now you can lift the whole piece off the mould and take a look. At this point you can use your rib to smooth down any creases from the newspaper on the inside of the bowl. Go round the whole piece and compress the surface and the rim with your rib.

STEP 8:

Trim the rim of the bowl with a knife and make sure the stand is flat to the table. You don't want it to wobble once it's fired, so take a look from all angles. You can press down on the bowl gently or trim the base with a knife to even it out.

STEP 9:

Scratch your initials onto the inside of the stand. Then leave for 5 days to go bone dry and fire your vase at cone 06 for 10 hours.

Glaze

For this pedestal bowl I have used a matt black glaze and the dipping technique. Use a jug to pour the glaze into the bowl, swirl it around to get full coverage with the glaze, then pour it back out. Then dip the pedestal bowl two-thirds of the way into the glaze, hold for 2 seconds and lift out. Wipe the glaze from the rim of the bowl with a wet sponge, then your piece can be fired one last time at cone 8 for 10 hours.

Vod vase

CLAY
– Craft crank stoneware
 10 × 500g (1lb 2oz)
 lumps

TOOLS
– Kitchen scales
– Rolling pin
– Rolling guides
– Ruler
– Two large ware boards
– Plastic sheet
– Metal rib
– Wooden tool
– Newspaper
– Grater (optional)
– Water and sponge

There's nothing more humbling than your body and mind actually failing you completely. I know what you're thinking, 'Keep it light, babes, this is pottery!' But this vase came about during a four-year period where mine did just that. This is particularly tough if you're proud like me and get actively cross when people offer to help. Being really sick for ages is akin to actual torture that I wouldn't wish on my worst enemies (you know who you are), but I did learn that failing is good, asking for help is a virtue, and vulnerability doesn't equal weakness. So put that on a sunset picture and post it on your socials.

Ultimately this vase reminds me of a really difficult time, during which I felt detached and incomplete. The hole in the vase was meant to represent those feelings of uselessness and inadequacy. Even the way I made the first vase was fraught with fragility and failure. But when I sat the finished piece on my shelf, looking at the hole in the vase actually felt like looking out at the sun streaming in through the opening of a cosy cave. The hole came to represent hope and comfort, and the vase resilience and strength. Illness is really hard, but it makes you tough. This is a hard vase to make, but if you can do it, nothing in ceramics will scare you.

STEP 1:

Bash your lumps of clay against the table into cubes, then use your rolling pin to bash, flip and roll into 8mm (⅓in) thick slabs. You are aiming to roll them out into four rhombus shapes around 14cm × 14cm (5½in × 5½in) and six rectangle shapes around 8cm × 25cm (3in × 10in). Lay the pieces out on your ware boards in order of which one you rolled first to last, then you can use them in this order later to ensure the drying time is relatively equal. Leave these ten flat pieces to stiffen up for roughly 30 minutes. We don't want them to go leather hard.

STEP 2:

After 30 minutes lay out a big sheet of plastic or a few cut-up plastic bags. Take each clay piece and bend it into a rough cylinder, then stand them on the plastic on their ends and leave for 30 minutes.

STEP 3:

Now the clay is harder it should be able to support itself while you build. Take the first rectangular slab you rolled and blend the edges together to make a cylinder. I don't use slip and score for this as the clay is still pretty wet. Just blend the clay with a wooden tool the same way we did with the coil pots. Blend it thoroughly inside and outside, then smooth over any cracks roughly with a rib.

TIP: Periodically spray the edges of the slabs that are waiting to be built so that they stay moist.

STEP 4:

Then take a rhombus piece (in order of dryness also) and seal that to one end of the cylinder as a corner piece. Blend with a wooden tool, then smooth it all down roughly with your rib. Then take another rhombus shape and attach it to the other end of the cylinder so that you have made what looks like a segment of a doughnut.

TIP: If the doughnut segment starts to collapse, take a few sheets of balled-up newspaper and stuff them inside as support; we can remove these later.

STEP 5:

Repeat step 4 with another rectangle and two rhombus shapes to make another segment. Now you should have two doughnut segments that you can join together with two of the remaining rectangle slabs (the other two rectangle slabs are for the neck of your vase and repairs and patching). Make two more cylinders and lay out your two doughnut segments and cylinders ready to join.

STEP 6:

Now you need to join all the pieces together to make a doughnut. This bit is pretty fiddly; you might need to pinch out some of the segments a bit to make them fit, or tear off pieces of your leftover rectangle piece to patch up segments that don't quite meet up. Remember, the vase is meant to be organic and primitive looking, so you aren't aiming for a perfect shape. If it's a weird-shaped doughnut, that's good.

STEP 7

Before you seal up the last piece, put your hands inside and check all the joins, smoothing down any areas that you missed. Make sure the doughnut is plump and full of air before sealing it over completely – the air is what's going to support the vase while it goes leather hard. When it comes to applying the last piece you will not be able to smooth down on the inside until later, so just use a large piece of spare slab and smooth down the outside. Look over and roughly smooth down the whole piece to make sure there are no cracks or holes from which air can escape. Use two ware boards on either side of the piece to flip it over and work on the other side without damaging it. Then leave the vase to go leather hard.

STEP 8:

You should have one cylinder left, which is going to be the neck of your vase. Seal this into a cylinder and leave under loose plastic to go soft leather hard.

STEP 9:

Now your vase is soft leather hard, it's time for the fun bit. You should be able to pick the whole thing up now and press it against your work bench to flatten out the sides to make it more square, or roll it to make it more round. It's also time to choose which way up you would like it to be, so try it out a few different ways to see what you think looks best. Flatten out the base by gently pressing it against your work bench. You will know if it is not dry enough to stand on its own because the sides of the vase will start to crack. If so, leave on its side for a little longer and go back in an hour or so to see if it will hold its own weight.

STEP 10:

Once leather hard, position the neck of the vase where you want it and cut a slightly smaller hole in the doughnut than the one in the neck. Pull up the extra clay into the neck and blend the neck to the vase inside and out. At this point you can look inside the vase and smooth down any visible unblended areas from the last piece to seal the doughnut earlier.

STEP 11:

Once you are happy with the shape of your vase, you can work on the finish with your metal rib. I like to scrape away the clay, leaving it rough in parts and smooth in others. Use a sponge to create a completely smooth finish, or a grater or metal rib for a rough finish.

STEP 12:

Make sure the bottom is flat and smooth it over, then scratch in your initials. Leave on a ware board for 5 days to go bone dry, then fire your vase at cone 06 degrees for 10 hours.

Glaze

For this vase I have used a matt white glaze and the pouring technique. Use a jug to pour the glaze into the vase, then quickly pick it up and rotate it as you tip out the glaze to get full coverage. Hold the vase over a bucket and pour glaze over two-thirds of the vase. Wait for this to dry, then pour glaze over the rest of the vase. I layer the glaze to make an abstract pattern and leave large parts of the vase unglazed. Wipe the glaze from the top of the neck of the vase and the bottom with a wet sponge. Fire one last time at cone 8 for 10 hours.

Little side table

CLAY

– Dracot stoneware
  4 × 2½kg (5½lb) lumps
  1.8kg (4lb) lump
  Matching slip

TOOLS

– Kitchen scales
– Rolling pin
– Ruler
– 15mm (½in) rolling guides
– Knife
– Plastic sheet
– Rib
– Large ware boards
– Pile of books
– Wooden tool
– Metal rib
– Water and sponge

You read it right, a side table made of clay. Unconventional? Yes. Too heavy? Maybe. As cool as your Nan's mid-century G Plan nest of tables? Totally. This table is just a big square slab pot, magically transformed into a table by turning it upside down. This one is going to be square, but you could try any shape really. The main thing you have to remember is that it needs to fit in the kiln, and that's why it's called a 'little side table'.

There are few things to bear in mind when embarking on this project. It's a big project that will take a couple of days, so make sure you have plenty of time set aside. You will also need a lot of space and there's a point when it will get quite messy, so set up somewhere that can accommodate this. It's worth going to the local hardware store and asking them to cut a sheet of plywood into five 36cm × 26cm (14in × 10in) ware boards or, if not, making sure you have at least the equivalent flat wooden surface to dry all five slabs on. It's really important that your slabs have the space and time to go properly leather hard. These are such large slabs they will be very difficult to handle if they are too soft and your whole piece could collapse. This project is all about the preparation.

STEP 1:

With some force, bash your lumps of clay against the table
into big cubes. Then bash them flatter with your rolling pin
as evenly as you can. Bash them on each side until you have
4cm (1½in) flat rectangles.

*TIP: To keep the rectangular shape you can lift and bash your slabs
on all four sides every now and again.*

STEP 2:

Now use 15mm (½in) rolling guides to roll your 2½kg
(5½lb) bashed-out rectangles into 34cm × 24cm (13in ×
9½in) slabs. Rolling out each slab on your prepared ware
boards will make it easier to judge the size. You can also
mark out the dimensions on your boards and wedge the
rolling guides up to the marks with clay to roll an even
slab. Roll out your 1.8kg (4lb) rectangle into a 24cm (9½in)
square and leave both for about 3 hours to go leather hard.

STEP 3:

Once leather hard, use a knife and a ruler to trim all four of your rectangular slabs to 33cm × 23cm (12½in × 9in). Go along the two long edges and one short edge at a 45-degree angle with your knife, leaving one short side flat. Keep all the trimmings straight and put them to one side sealed in a piece of plastic to use later. Score all the edges you have just cut at a 45-degree angle. Trim your square slab down to 23cm (9in) square. Cut all four edges at a 45-degree angle with your knife and score all the cut edges.

STEP 4:

Mix up a big batch of slip and daub it onto one side of two of your rectangle slabs. With one slab flat on a ware board, lift the other slab on a board at a right angle and press into position. With one hand supporting the clay and the other on the board, press down onto the flat slab until you see all the slip oozing out. Then place a pile of books against the ware board to hold the slab in place. Repeat this on the other side and support with more books, then wait for 20 minutes for the slip to dry.

STEP 5:

Daub slip along the long edges of the final rectangular slab and the edges you are going to fix it to. Lift the fourth long side of the table into place and, supporting it underneath with your hand, run your wooden tool over the joins until slip oozes out. Leave for 10 minutes for the slip to dry.

TIP: You may need to use more books to support this final piece and stop it bowing in the middle.

STEP 6:

Using the ware boards, very carefully lift the four rectangle slabs to a standing position. Daub slip along all the edges of the remaining square slab and the edges on the top of the cuboid. Lift the square slab into place on top of the cuboid and use a board to gently press it down until the slip oozes out.

STEP 7:

Use a rib to remove excess slip and use your wooden tool to blend all the joins together. Now retrieve your trimmings from earlier and use these instead of coils to reinforce all the joins on the inside. You'll notice they're cut in nice right angles and fit flush into the joins. Blend the trimmings into the joins with your wooden tool.

STEP 8:

Then go over the entire piece with your metal rib to
scrape away the surface of the clay and create a coarse
edge. And because I dislike uniformity of any kind I've
used the metal tool to gouge out some shallow chunks and
make irregular marks.

STEP 9

Make sure the bottom and top of your table are flat and
smoothed over, and scratch your initials on the inside.
Then leave drying upside down with a loose layer of plastic
for 1 day, turn the right way up and dry for a further 4 days
to go bone dry. Fire your table at cone 06 degrees for 10
hours.

Glaze

*For this table I have used a mustard speckle glaze and the dipping
method. Dip the table into a bucket of glaze a third of the way in,
hold for 2 seconds and lift out. Wipe any glaze from the bottom with
a wet sponge and fire one last time at cone 8 for 10 hours.*

Resources

OPEN-ACCESS STUDIOS

UK

www.turningearth.org

www.thekilnrooms.com

www.studio-pottery-london.com

www.glasgowceramicstudio.com

US

www.gasworksnyc.com

www.sculpturespacenyc.com

www.clayca.com

www.thepotterystudio.com

www.claybythebaysf.com

Germany

www.kleistonestudio.com

www.claygroundceramics.com

www.peaceoutparadise.com

Spain

www.atuell.com

The Netherlands

www.studiopansa.com

Australia

www.classbento.com.au

www.clayground.com.au

BOOKS

Material Science for the Potters
W.G. Lawrence

Making Pots
Stefan Andersson

Clay
Contemporary Ceramic Artisans

Mastering Hand Building
Sunshine Cobb

A Way of Living
Herman Miller

The Beauty of Everyday Things
Soetsu Yanagi

MATERIALS

General
www.claycellar.co.uk

www.bathpotters.co.uk

www.potclays.co.uk

Starter tool set
www.bathpotters.co.uk

Vulcan stoneware medium
www.potclays.co.uk

Craft crank stoneware
www.potclays.co.uk

Draycot white stoneware
www.potclays.co.uk

Decorating slip
www.potclays.co.uk

Brush-on glazes
www.potclays.co.uk

Ready mixed glaze
www.potclays.co.uk

Air dry clay
www.glsed.co.uk

MAKERS

Jacqueline de la Fuente – @delajardin

Giuseppe Parrinello – @giuseppeparrinelloceramics

Alena Peschek – @alena_peschek_studio

Claire Wan – @wan.ceramics

Libby Hood – @hoodceramics

Boys Do Ceramics – @boysdoceramics

Åslund Tsang – @aaslund.tang

Yasmin Bawa – @yasmin_bawa

Laurence Leenaert – @lrnce

Nicola Gillis – @nicolagillis

Lalese Stamps – @lollylollyceramics

Jack Kabangu – @jaackkabangu

Nana Sacko – @shopsacko

Liv and Dom Cave-Sutherland – @livanddom

Bisila Noha – @bisilanoha

Phoebe Collings-James – @phoebethegorgon

Sherród Faulks – @deepblack.design

Tasha Reneé – @tashathrowsraw

Adele Brydges – @adelebrydges

Index

Acknowledgements

In what was a period of considerable and scary change in my life, being approached to write a book seemed like a bizarre, unreal dream. In the midst of a storm, a project so massive could have been what finally broke me, but in fact the opposite has turned out to be true. I'd go as far to say it's been the making of me, and I'm so grateful to have been given the opportunity by the lovely people at Kyle books to share my bad jokes and chunky pots with you all.

Making and photographing 24 ceramic pieces in what turned out to be the hottest summer on record, in a glass-roofed studio (so a greenhouse yeah?) is no mean feat. Luckily I had the dream team of my editor Samhita Foria and photographer Sarah Weal to keep me pepped up, on task and periodically change the ice pack taped to my butt. Collaborating with two such brilliant and talented women has been amazing. In eyebrow-searing heats they were both brimming with ideas and energy that turned what could have been a harrowing experience into outrageous fun and together we created a book I am really proud of.

While we're thanking women, thanks to all the pioneering, relentless, badass female makers and business women who were already out there slogging it to make gorgeous stuff for us and inspired me to take the plunge.

Holly, David, Lucas and Lester you gave me more LOLs, love and confidence than I deserve. I couldn't have done it without you guys feeding, watering, homing, stroking and caring for me, while asking for nothing in return. Thanks to all my family and friends and Joe, whose enduring belief in me is as touching as it is misguided. Especially my sister whose deafening unrelenting cheerleading got me writing every day. And of course to Mum and Dad, I can only apologise, you guys are just swell, stay sexy.